W. ROYCE ADAMS

AGAINST *the* Current

LITTLE RIPPLINGS AND SPUMINGS

ISBN: 979-8-9909378-0-2 (Paperback)
        979-8-9909378-1-9 (E-book)

Library of Congress Control Number: 2024913944

Published By:

Santa Barbara, CA 93103
www.rjkbooks.com

Publisher Provider:

Fiction writers, at least in their braver moments, do desire the truth: to know it, speak it, serve it. But they go about it in a peculiar and devious way, which consists in inventing persons, places, and events which never did and never will exist or occur, and telling about these fictions in detail and at length and with great deal of emotion, and then when they are done writing down this pack of lies, they say, There! That's the truth!

—Ursula K. Le Guin, *The Left Hand of Darkness*

ACKNOWLEDGEMENTS

"Blue Haze" appeared in COE REVIEW, Vol. 47, Spring 2016

CONTENTS

RIPPLINGS

You can barely see it now, thanks to tight stitches, aging skin and eyeglasses, but there is a small scar across the bridge of my nose that as a teenager I wore with much pride, a badge of honor, as I saw it. But of all the scars my body bears today, and there are many, this one was, without a doubt, incurred among the most brainless of circumstances.

When I was sixteen, I was fortunate enough to obtain a part-time job working after school and on Saturdays at Tri City Grocery. My tasks were uncomplicated, but varied enough to keep me from getting bored. I loaded and unloaded trucks of assorted canned goods and crates of produce. I stamped and shelved every can and box that needed a price on it. I trimmed and water sprayed produce making sure it looked fresh, then displayed my work in colorful arrangements for the customers just like you see in stores today. I scrubbed the warehouse area in the back and hosed down the sidewalk in the front of the store. I bagged customers' groceries at checkout, sometimes carrying their purchases out to their cars. I even spied on customers when requested to do so. Eventually, I reached my goal: I became a cashier.

At first, there was only one negative I associated with the job. Even though a part-timer, I had to join the retail groceries union, which took money out of my pennies-an-hour pay envelope every week, and was forced to attend union meetings once a month or be fined.

But I digress. Let's get back to the scar.

When I was hired, another teenager already worked there. Zack, about my age and size, and a school dropout, held ambitions that he would be hired full time some day. However, with my being hired, he could see his dream fading, so resentment toward me could be seen in his icy blues from day one.

Dave, the store manager, always seen wearing a clean white apron and tilted paper butcher's cap, told Zack when I was hired to "show him the ropes." I soon realized the only ropes Zack wanted to show me were ones that would go around my neck.

One of his first tasks was to show me how to cut open cardboard boxes of canned goods so the boxes could be used for customer use, storing items or trash containers. Done right, the cans inside would slip out easily for price stamping. It seemed easy enough, except Zack waited until I had finished stamping two boxes of canned goods and placing them on the shelf before telling me that the stamped price was wrong. He, of course, had set the rubber ink stamp himself. With a false smile, he admitted to his "mistake," but it was left to me to take all the cans off the shelf, separate the ones I had stamped from the ones already on the shelf, and re-stamp the correct price. By that time, the ink was set on the cans, so I had to take a marking pen to smudge out the wrong price and stamp the right price on the other end of the can. While doing this, Dave came down the aisle and saw me sitting on the floor surrounded by cans.

"How's it going? Problem?"

Before I had a chance to say a word, Zack said, "He stamped the wrong price on the cans."

I felt my face burn, expecting to get some kind of reprimand, while wanting to use the stamp on Zack's forehead.

Dave nodded to me. "Can you fix it?"

My dry voice managed, "Yes, sir. I'm marking out the wrong price and stamping on…"

"Okay, okay. But hurry it up. We're getting a truck load of produce in about fifteen minutes we're going to have to unload quickly."

He took off down the aisle and disappeared.

"You want to help me with this?" I asked Zack.

"Sorry. Can't. Have to do something out back before the truck comes."

Thanks to the Grocery Store Gods, who must have felt compassion for me, I managed to finish just when the truck arrived for unloading.

Because of the physical location of the store, there was no loading zone in back. Everything had to be taken through the front door to the back storeroom. That was the main reason Dave wanted us to hurry and get the truck delivery in the store.

Dave met Zack and me at the truck and gave Zack a list with numbers of the boxes and cartons we were to remove from the truck and place in the warehouse in the back of the store.

"Here," Dave pointed at the list Zack held. "Put these items behind those in the warehouse. We'll want to use those first."

"Right," Zack said.

Dave left us to our task.

We worked quickly getting things off the truck and stacking them by the front door. Zack looked at the list and then found certain numbers on the crates.

"Here," he pointed. "These two here and these three there go in first. Can you handle it? I need to take a leak. Be right back."

None of the cartons could be carried by hand. They had to be wheeled in on a dolly.

Wanting to show Dave I wasn't a complete flake, I made great time taking the indicated crates one by one to the back.

I was finished bringing in the cartons when Zack came back with another dolly. The two of us were quick and removed all the crates from the front of the store.

Once in the back, Zack said, "What's this?"

"What?"

"These crates. They're supposed to be in the front. You've got them stacked behind."

"You told me to bring these in first."

"No, idiot. Look at the list. These numbers go in front."

"That's not what you told me."

"Yes, I did. The numbers don't lie."

I knew damn well he had pulled another of his little pranks to make me look bad. But I fumed in silence and rearranged the cartons. No way was I going to run to Dave complaining my first week of work.

Zack's twisted little gambits continued that week and the next. He might send me to the warehouse in back to get a box of sixteen-ounce cans of tomatoes or some such, only to tell me that what I brought him was the wrong one. Then I had to go back for the "right" carton. Once he "accidentally" ran over my foot with a loaded dolly. Another time I heard him tell Dave I was "a slow worker" and that he "sometimes had to make up for it."

The end of his gambit came when we were both trimming lettuce in the back. The knives we used were like miniature Saracen swords, single edged blade, curved, very thin and very sharp. Zack started throwing his bad trim cuttings into my clean basket of lettuce ready to go on display.

"Hey! Knock it off." I said, throwing out his mess into his basket.

He got up and kicked my basket of lettuce on the floor.

You've heard of the tipping point? That was my tipping point—and apparently his.

I stood up. "Pick that up." It wasn't intended, but I held my knife as though I was going to attack him.

"Or what, huh?"

He either thought I was going to assault him, or he wanted to attack me. Maybe both. For whatever reason, he jabbed his knife at me, missing. I tried to read the look on his face. Was he challenging me? Was this for real?

Yes.

I left what I normally thought of as me suspended somewhere, and out stepped another part of me I'd never met before. The idea of cutting Zack became appealing. Assuming the role, I lunged at him, missing. He lunged, missed. Our movements were dance-like, nothing they'd teach at Arthur Murray's, just two performers keeping at each other, trying to outdo the other, moving in circles, jabbing forward, arching back, until the look on his face changed and he abruptly lowered his knife, staggering back with a startled look of surprise and shock.

While I hadn't felt the cut, the blood streamed down my nose, cheeks and chin, bringing both of us back to what little sense we never had to begin with.

I just stood there in a bleeding daze.

Zack, awakening to what he'd done, grabbed some paper towels from the restroom nearby.

"Here." He shoved them at me, hoping, I think, that the towels would make it all go away.

By now, the blood had dripped down on the chest part of my apron and my nose started throbbing with my pulse.

Zack just stood there, muttering, "Shit, shit, shit."

"You cut me!" I said, letting the obvious occur to me for real.

"We're gonna get fired," Zack said, which wasn't *my* first thought, but the truth of it sank in.

"Goodbye job" seemed fairly sure, but I also knew I needed a band aid or something for my nose, so I realized there was no way to keep this from Dave. I had no choice but to go to Dave's little office hoping he had a First Aid kit.

When he saw me, his eyes told me it would be best if I didn't look in the mirror.

"What the hell happened to you?" He took the bloody towels away from my nose. "Jesus. You need stitches, not a band-aid. How'd this happen?"

As easy as becoming a knife dancer, the liar in me came to the fore. "Accident. I asked Zack to throw me a can of cleanser, but the edge of the can hit my nose before I could catch it."

No, I didn't say this to be all noble and protect Zack. I selfishly didn't want to lose my job if I could help it. It seemed a plausible lie.

The way he looked at me I'm not sure Dave wanted to know any more than that. He gave me some gauze pads for my nose, sent me to a nearby doctor, told me the union would pay for it, and that I should go home and he'd see me tomorrow if I felt okay.

Those sweet words: "see me tomorrow" made the lying worth it.

Zack was standing nearby so he knew the story I'd told. I felt certain he would verify it if Dave asked.

For a few days at school, my bandaged nose brought me some attention. What happened to your nose? A knife fight? Wow! How many stitches? Does it hurt? Who'd you fight? As Mark Twain would say, I imagine I made a few "stretches" in my answers.

As for my parents, they believed the story I told Dave.

When I returned to work, Zack didn't exactly apologize, but in his awkward way thanked me for saving both our butts. I never let him know my intentions had nothing to do with him when I told Dave what happened. But things did change at work. Zack no longer needed to show me his ropes and we learned to tolerate each other.

And when the bandage came off and that scar stood out, I wore my battle scar proudly.

Little did I know then of the real scars yet to come.

* * * * *

I hurried along the long hall smelling the freshly painted green student lockers looking for Room 201. Squeezing the key in my hand, I couldn't help but smile. Room 201, my very own classroom. About to put all those years of college courses and training to use, I felt proud and eager, along with a touch of trepidation. Yes, I'd finally made it—a high school English teacher, a professional.

I found Room 201 near the end of the hall, but I didn't need the key. The door stood propped open with a student desk chair. I peered in the doorway and lost my smile.

The chalkboard along the front wall tilted down to one side, attached only at the top of one end. Conspicuous black and red wires twisted out from the wall above the slanted chalkboard where I assumed a clock should be. A bulletin board, not yet mounted, leaned along a sidewall. Masking tape framed the row of smudged windowpanes on the opposite wall. Stacked 12 × 12inch floor tiles waited to be set in one unfinished corner. The student desk chairs, shoved together into another corner, hid my desk.

I again checked the room number above the door. 201. Yes, my assigned room. Why hadn't the office told me the room wasn't ready? I stepped inside and flicked the light switch. At least the lights worked. I checked my watch. Twenty minutes until classes began. "Okay," I told myself, "you're a professional now. Take charge."

I pulled the desk chairs apart and arranged them in a circle, planning to try a method learned in one of my college courses that could help me quickly memorize all the students' names. The first student would introduce him or herself, then the student next to her would repeat that student's name and her own name. The student next to that one would repeat her name, the previous student's name, and then state his or her name, and so on around the circle so that the last person had to remember everyone's name that came before. I served as the last one in the circle and that way would know most of their names.

I tried to arrange the chairs so that no one would be near the leaning bulletin board or the unfinished floor. The chalkboard looked too dangerous to touch, so I didn't write my name or any class information on it. I didn't see any chalk anyway. I stood wondering what else I could do to make the room look more attractive.

"This 201?"

Startled, I twisted around too fast, tangling my foot in the legs of a student desk chair. When I tried to shake loose, I lost my balance hopping on one foot, then crashed into the leaning bulletin board, taking it to the floor with me.

I lay with mouth open, looking up at the amused face of my very first student.

"Uh—yes—this is 201. Can I…" I tried pushing the heavy board off, "…help you?" A ludicrous question, I thought, considering my position.

"Yeah." He looked down on me and flashed his blue student registration card. "I'm early, huh?"

"You're the first," I said, crawling out from under the bulletin board.

He moved to help push it back against the wall so I could get up. "You the teacher?"

"Yes," I grunted, struggling up, then brushing off my clothes and telling him my name. I almost offered to shake his hand, but caught myself. I stood as tall as I could, but our eyes remained level.

I could tell he was sizing me up and didn't see me as a threat. He was tanned, had thick black hair slicked back with plenty of hair oil, a small earring in one ear and the faint beginning of a mustache. He wore a tight, white T-shirt revealing a muscled body, Levis rolled up at the cuffs, colorful argyle socks and Penny loafers. Something told me he wasn't going to like my class.

"Where should I sit?"

"Anywhere. Take your pick." I waved my arm around the circle of chairs. That's when I noticed the pain in my wrist.

The student slouched into a seat. "New here, huh?"

"Why do you say that?" I rubbed my wrist, pain building, wondering if it was broken or just sprained.

"The chairs." He broke eye contact, stretched his neck around in the direction of the circle of desks.

"The chairs?"

"Yeah. Seems like every new teacher puts our desks in a circle. I don't want to be the last one and have to repeat all the names." He looked at me. "Want my card?" He held out his registration card, but before I could take it a loud voice boomed out behind me.

"Hey, there! Who put them chairs like that?"

I turned, carefully this time, to face a burly man with his hands on his hips. A Dodgers' baseball cap pushed back on his head revealed a round, pink, scowling face. His forest green shirt, losing a battle against his stomach, spilled over his oversized belt that held up a pair of matching green pants. For security, I suppose, he also wore blue and red suspenders. A huge batch of keys hung importantly at his side.

"Excuse me?"

"Them chairs." He pointed, stuck out his chin and peered at me. "Oh, you're new. Right," he stated. "Look, here's how it works. The chairs has got to be set up in a certain order, see? Let me show you." He proceeded to undo the circle.

"See those brown tiled squares here? Well, a row of chairs goes like this here on the brown tile squares on Monday so I can sweep the tan row of tiles here." He pointed. "On Tuesday, I move those chairs over to this row of tan tile squares so's I can sweep the brown tiles." He moves and points. "Then on Wednesday, I move 'em back to Monday's row of brown and sweep Tuesday's row of tan and so on down the line. Now you got them all mixed up. Slows me down on my rounds."

"Ah, yes, well, I see your routine, but…I…" Wait. Am I supposed to take orders from a custodian? "Look," I told him, "today I'd like to have the students sit in a circle. Besides, when I got here the chairs were all bunched up in a corner. Look around. The room's a mess. See, some tiles still need to be laid." I pointed in their direction.

"Yeah, well, workers can't start until eight o five. Union, ya' know. And suit yourself about them chairs, but I want 'em on the right tiles end of the day."

Before I could form a proper response, the custodian was gone and my audience was filing in. Several of the students looked apprehensive, stepping back out of the room to check the number against their class schedules. I tried to hold a smile and reassure them with "good mornings" and "have a seat" while re-forming the circle of desks. The bell to start class rang before I could finish. I felt slight relief when some of the students, knowing the routine, helped.

Taking a deep breath, I stood in the middle of the circle and announced in a quivering voice, "Welcome to 10th grade English." I cleared my throat and reached for a deeper, solid tone and stated my name. "Please pass your registration cards to—what's your name?" I pointed to my early student.

"Tony."

"To Tony. I have an information sheet for you to fill out. Put your…" Before I could finish, one very tall man and one very short one reminding me of the cartoon characters Mutt and Jeff barged into the room, rattling their tool boxes.

"Don't let us bother you," Mutt drawled, dropping his toolbox in time with Jeff. "We're here to finish up the room. Won't take long."

I nodded and began passing out the forms to the students and giving directions. But the noisy workmen drew most of their interest. Jeff grunted pig-like as he lifted up the unattached end of the chalkboard to hold while Mutt's loud electric drill whined screw holes in it and the wall.

I didn't actually see it happen. At that moment, my back was turned to all the noise. But I did hear the chalkboard fall, the workmen curse, and the students' responses. When I turned, I saw Tony's argyle socks and Penny loafers sticking out from under the fallen chalkboard, a less colorful version of the Wicked Witch of the East having a house fall on her.

The workmen lifted the board off just as I got to him.

"Jeez, I'm sorry kid. The damn thing got away from me," Jeff said squatting beside Tony.

"Are you all right?" I asked the boy.

Tony lay on the floor, eyes open, but glassy looking. A little blood oozed from his temple.

I tried again. "Are you all right, Tony?"

Still no answer.

"Jeez, kid. I'm really sorry," Jeff said. "I'm sure somebody's insurance will cover this." He looked at me. Do I need insurance for this?

Curious students formed a crowd. Mutt and I kept asking Tony if he could talk, but he gave no response. Finally, he moved to sit up and they helped him lean against the wall. I wasn't sure he should be moved, but I was relieved to see he looked alive.

"Maybe we should get him to the nurse's office," I suggested. The workman Jeff, probably out of guilt, volunteered to take him.

Once they left, I had everyone sit again as I began walking around inside the circle answering questions and making certain the forms were being filled out correctly, my mind half taken with worry about Tony.

Then the class and I smelled it.

I hoped it would be ignored, but a student had to ask. "Whew! What's that stink?"

"Hey, Mickey, you let that one?" someone else called out, causing snickers and giggles.

Everyone began to look at each other suspiciously when Mutt spoke up. "Sorry about the smell, folks. This glue for the floor tiles smells like cat piss when you first open the can. Won't take long to finish up here."

One of the students asked if he could open a window, which I certainly had no objection to his doing. The high windows required a special pole with an attachment on the end that hooked into the window latches. The boy did a fine job considering some of the window frames had been freshly painted and tended to stick. But when he turned away from the windows to put the pole away, he accidentally smacked a girl's jaw with one end.

Her wailing started on a low note and then crescendoed into a high, sustained cacophony of inventive tones. With the help of her girlfriends and me, the student finally calmed down to quiet, sobbing moans. I sent her to the nurse's office to have her slowly swelling jaw examined.

After she left, and wondering if this was all really happening to me, I tried to get the class back to completing the forms. But Mutt, finished setting the tiles, excused himself and walked through the diminishing circle of chairs with a ladder and set it up under the wires sticking from the wall. All watched as he held the new clock in one arm and took one step at a time up the ladder.

"Okay, class. Enough clock gazing. Let's finish up those forms." I tried to sound as if I were still in charge. But soon more giggles began with pointing and nods toward the clock. I looked and saw the clock hands spinning around as if time didn't want to behave.

Puzzled, Mutt leaned back from the ladder to see what was wrong. He leaned back too far.

In truth, his fall touched on the comical at first, and their immediate reaction brought out nervous laughter. But the workman's expletives brought everyone up short. Between every other foul word it became clear Mutt thought he had broken his leg.

What was I to do but ask a couple of the bigger boys to help the poor man to the nurse's office.

Things quieted down again and the students finally finished the information forms. I began sending students two at a time to the book room, as I had been instructed to do earlier, but they came back informing me that the books for my classes had not arrived. Next week, maybe, they were told.

Before I had time to realize how that might affect my teaching plans, the nurse came in with several forms for me to sign. One triplicate set, the nurse said, explained how the boy Tony had received his concussion by being hit on the head with a bulletin board.

"Are you sure that's how it happened?" the nurse asked. "The man who brought the boy up tried to explain it, but it seemed, well, far-fetched."

I read and signed the report assuring the nurse that to the best of my knowledge it correctly explained how it happened.

"Well, if you say so. Incidentally, I had to send the girl hit in the jaw to the dentist, so she won't be back today either." She handed me the forms to sign explaining that event.

"And the workman?" I was afraid to ask.

"Oh, leg's broken, I'm sure. Fractured tibia's my guess. His co-worker took him to the hospital." She handed me another set of papers regarding that accident. "Busy day you've had here," she commented, a slight smile that turned me against her. "If you plan to have classes like this often, let me know. I'll move my office closer."

"Very funny." I faked a smile and signed.

When the bell rang that finally ended my first day as a professional, it didn't take long for the students to disappear. I stood alone in my classroom with the chairs now facing all directions, the unusable bulletin board still leaning against the wall, the chalk board no longer even halfway up, the piss-like stench still in my nostrils, and the hands on the clock running mad as one hand chased the other.

"Don't forget to line the chairs up," the custodian reminded me as he passed the door.

I knew it wasn't professional, but frustration won the day. I reached up and slammed shut the nearest window. My hand went through a pane, shattering the glass and returning the ache to my wrist.

Standing there watching my blood drip on one of Tuesday's tan tiles, my wrist throbbing with every red drop, I knew I should go to the nurse's office.

Or, maybe just bleed to death?

Anxious is an appropriate catchword for how I felt about my first high-school parent-teacher conference night. Throw in tense and uneasy, even though I prepared for the event with carefully proofread handouts explaining my literature course plus a special file folder for each student's test scores, homework and grades. I printed my name and class title on the blackboard so parents wandering the halls would know they'd reached the right room. New at this, I think I hid my nervousness from my first two scheduled appointments and came off as someone who knew what he was doing. At least those parents thanked me when they left and let me know their offspring were enjoying the class. I began feeling a bit more confident and optimistic.

When my third appointment arrived, she just stood at the door and I couldn't help but be struck by her attractiveness. She wore a solid black form-fitting dress that emphasized a trim figure. A long string of pearls stood out against her dark attire. A large, black leather purse hung from one shoulder. She wore high heels putting her eye level the same as mine. Her short blonde hair framed an unsmiling face that belied her overall pleasant appearance. She didn't come in right away, and I wondered if she was at the wrong classroom or waiting to be invited in.

So I did. "Good evening. Please come in. Have a seat."

The moment she entered my classroom her anger at something showed, and her harsh tone of voice caught me off guard.

"Lyle tells me you're the one who gave him this book to read."

She searched in her purse, pulled out a paperback book and waved it like a flag at a rally.

Oh, oh. This did not bode well. Something's coming, something big…

Her narrowed eyes barely gave away their blue, but they gave me the prickly feeling she was not here to thank me.

"Yes, ma'am. I did."

Well, I wasn't going to lie about it. I did loan him the book. And it looked like my goodwill gesture backfired…what did that little bastard tell her…

"You should be ashamed of yourself. Why would you do such a thing?"

First-year-teacher me thought with some pride that I'd awakened her son to the joys of reading. When Lyle told me with smugness that he'd reached his senior year in school and managed never to read a novel, I loaned him the book betting him he'd want to finish it.

Still waving the book, she began what I soon assumed was a botched attempt at a speech she had prepared but was having trouble remembering the exact memorized word order.

"Why…I want to know…why would you give this book to a teenager? It's a…it's a…filthy book. The words…the words are…are disgusting." She held the book between thumb and forefinger as if the physical book itself were dirty. She shook her head and closed her eyes for emphasis. "It's a disgusting book. Revolting. When I saw my boy reading this…four letter words…nasty four-letter words every page. Do you, as a treeacher…ah…teacher con… condone such language?"

Oh, piss on a poodle! The woman's been drinking. This is not going to be easy.

"It's like you're telling my boy it's okay to say such words. It's pornographic. It's vilish. I'm going to your principal with this. You shouldn't be allowed to teach such filth."

I felt my blood heating up and my stunned brain scrambling for a defense. I tried not to sound as taken aback as I was. How do I defend myself against this unexpected rant?

"Look," I tried to tell her, "I'm not teaching the book in class. I gave it to Lyle to read because I thought he would relate to it and get him interested in…"

"Relate to it? My son, relate to this…this distashful trash?"

She dangled the "distashful" book closer to my face, forcing me to lean back from its familiar simple cover, mostly red with an inlaid pencil-like drawing of a wild, galloping carousel horse, the title in yellow letters at the top, the author's name in black letters at the bottom. Until then, I never realized how much fury the cover portrayed.

Now I could smell the alcohol and a tinge of cigarette. This wasn't fair. She'd prepared herself for this encounter with a martini or two. It left me at a disadvantage. None of the too numerous, mostly absurd time-wasted education classes I had been forced to take in order to get my General Secondary Teaching Credential provided insight on how to handle angry, inebriated mothers during parent-teacher conferences. I was alone in my classroom with a fuming, shouting, tipsy woman without a clue as to how to proceed.

My inner dialogue bellowed, *"Who the fuck do you think you are, Mrs. Turpin?"* while my counter dialogue winced, *"You're done for, buddy. Watch your step. She probably has connections and you're going to be fired your first year of teaching. You should have stayed in the navy. What made you think you could teach?"*

"I meant no harm," I said in simple-minded feeble self-defense. *Damn you, lady, damn you!*

"The harm's been done. You've…you've turned my son against me."

Bull shit, lady. I think you had a head start on that one. I've only had your kid in class for a month.

"Now he hates me because I took this dreadful book away from him."

Oh, poor mother boohoo you. Careful. Control your malice. Come on, counter with something.

"Have you read the book?" I asked, searching for a life buoy.

"Read it? Of course not. Why, why would I want to read it if I don't want my son reading it? I'd never seen him reading a book before. I had to see what it was. It was enough just to flip through the pages and see the filth."

"But the book is about a teenage boy, like Lyle, struggling to find himself…"

"You think my son needs to find himself? He's not lost. He knows who he is."

You're full of crap, lady! He's one of the most lost students I have. He's trying to find out who he is by acting out. Just come to class and watch your son in action. I've had to call him on behavior several times. He reminds me of Holden. He's smart, but over sensitive and has trouble relating to classmates. He might, like Holden, end up on a shrink's couch. That's another reason I gave him the book.

I wanted to say all that, but instead I tried reason. "I can understand you have trouble with the language, but the author's not condoning it. He's attempting to be honest in his portrayal of a sensitive teenage boy, to show his confusion, grief and need for love."

"Love?" Her voice went up an octave. "Show me any love in this book. Prostitutes. Vile sex."

Maybe if you read the book, you stupid witch, you'd see it. No, on second thought, you never would understand.

This was going nowhere, and I felt I'd stepped on an exploding brain mine.

You're not in Kansas anymore, buddy boy.

"What would you like me to do?"

"Well, what do you think? Quit passing out filthy books to your students. Who knows what other, who knows—what junk—you've given to other students. Well, I intend to stop you. Oh, yes. You don't belong in the classroom. We'll just see…yes, we'll just see what the…what the principal has to say about all this."

She threw the book at me, turned and left the room, bumping in to the doorframe as she left. She gave out a little cry and I hoped to hell she'd hurt herself. Her purse strap slipped off her shoulder and the purse fell to the floor. She glared back at me and I wondered if her look meant I was rude for not picking it up for her, or she felt embarrassment at her staggering exit, or just her last hateful shot across the bow.

You drunken bitch! I was wrong! You're not at all attractive!

I picked the book off the floor feeling my classroom was left tainted with bile. Before I had time to think about what just happened and what was going to happen to me, the parents of my next scheduled conference arrived. If they overheard anything, they didn't let on. At least they brought smiles and their friendly demeanor helped subdue the vitriol enveloping me.

After introductions, my student Steven's mother noticed the book on my desk and picked it up.

Crap! Here we go again…

"Oh. Are you going to teach this in your class? We gave Steven a copy for his birthday and he loved it."

Oh, you wonderful, wonderful lady! Would your husband mind if I kissed you?

With that small boost, I somehow managed to refocus on the task at hand and made it through the rest of the evening conferences with no more threats of being fired.

But I also made a written note of the names of Steven's parents just in case witnesses for the defense needed to be called in my trial.

"No, no, we're not selling; we're placing."

I listened as Max, my training supervisor, explained to the young couple sitting cornered on their stained living room sofa that he and I were not selling encyclopedias. No, no. We were marketing researchers. Our job was to seek out parents who showed concern and interest in their children's education. The company we represented authorized us to place the entire set, all twenty volumes, in the homes of qualified families—for free. That's right, free. As market researchers, our job entailed finding families who would guarantee the use of the encyclopedias once placed in a home.

I looked at the uncomfortable parents. Late twenties, I guessed. Close to my own age at the time. The husband, caught off guard, had just come home from work and found Max and me already there. His blue overalls were covered with dirt and grease. Looking tired and wary, he kept leaning forward, then back, glancing often at his wife with a why-did-you-do-this-to-me look. The thin wife, hair in curlers, showed real interest in receiving a free set of encyclopedias for her children, but didn't seem to appreciate it would be years before her kids could read them. Their runny-nosed, diapered two-year-old daughter kept trying to climb her mother's body and pull her away, whining "Mommy, come. Mommy, come."

Their four-year-old son, arms outstretched for wings, kept vrooming through the house making loud dive-bombing noises when he flew near me. When he noticed I was avoiding his bombing runs, he decided to strafe me with machine-gun fire. He soon ran out of bullets and I won the war.

During my three-day training session, I had learned verbatim all that Max explained to the couple. "To qualify, all you have to do is promise to keep the set up-to-date by buying each annual supplemental volume that includes all the discoveries and new information for each year. Without the annual supplement, the twenty volumes would become dated. Are you willing to keep the set up to date?"

I now knew the routine and the pitch. Tomorrow I'd be going out on my own.

Max handed the husband a sample volume and pointed out its superior features: the binding and stitching quality, the sturdy faux-leather cover, and the way the two-page maps aligned evenly when opened. "And here," Max pointed out, "just look at this colored drawing of Icarus. Kids love this stuff."

The husband took the book with reluctance, nodded, flipped through some pages without showing interest, then handed it to his wife. The two-year-old tried to take it from her.

"No, no. Mustn't touch," the mother said, holding the volume high, trying to exam it while she fought having her dress pushed up over her thighs by small, sticky fingers.

"Hey, now," the husband said. He reached over and pulled his wife's dress down.

I shifted about, not comfortable in this picture. I wasn't sure I was cut out to be a market researcher, but I needed the job. A high school teacher at the time, I didn't earn enough to sustain my growing family. I had struggled along for two years now, hoping I wouldn't have to supplement my meager teaching salary. I loved teaching; it was all I wanted to do. But I needed to make some money.

The newspaper ad I had answered offered openings in market research as a way to supplement income. It sounded appealing. I could still teach and not have to worry about taking a job with regular hours. The job would allow me to work as many evenings as I wanted, plus a placement of just one set of encyclopedias a week would help keep the family finances afloat.

Like a mantra during my training, I had heard, "It's win, place, and show. You are not selling encyclopedias. You are not sales people. It's important that you understand that. We need you to show our product around, to familiarize people with our name, and to place this educational tool with parents who will use it. Everyone wins when you place what you show." During the training sessions, I had convinced myself that placing encyclopedias could be considered an extension of teaching, a way to take learning into people's homes.

Now, my first day going into those homes, I was witnessing "marketing research" at work. I had to admit Max was good at it. If he succeeded with this couple, it would be his third "placement" of the day.

"Now, for us to place a set in your home all you have to do is promise to buy each yearly supplement for only $39.95." Max's tone and facial expressions hinted at a deal not to be passed up. I wondered if he practiced in front of a mirror.

"I thought you said the encyclopedias was free." The husband smiled as if he'd tripped up Max.

"The set is." Max looked hurt. "The entire twenty volumes are free. Twenty volumes. You're just promising to buy the yearly supplement to keep the set updated. Now I consider that quite a deal. If you were to buy this set, it would cost you hundreds of dollars. But we're not selling. Of course, if you're not interested, then I've made a mistake about your qualifications."

The husband chewed his lip, looked at his wife, then back at Max. "You mean, for just $39.95, we get the entire set?" the husband asked as he gave his wife a what-do-you-think look.

Max smiled his practiced now-isn't-that-an-unbelievable-deal look, then added, "Like I said, just promise you'll use the set—and that you'll keep it current through the yearly supplements."

"Gotta be a catch. You're not gonna let us have a whole set of these for that price." The husband leaned forward, elbows on his knees. Then he picked up the sample Volume VII and handled it without really looking at it.

I could see him sinking into Max's pitch.

"No catch, sir." Max tilted his head, looking hurt again. "Look, for us, you're free advertising. When your neighbors and friends see the set and hear how you and your children use it for school reports and such, why, they'll want to buy their own. Then that's where we'll make our money. They'll have to pay for the entire set that you get for free."

I noticed the husband looked at his wife for guidance. He was weakening. The wife picked up the runny-nosed kid, now pulling on the mother's ear and making jungle-bird screeching noises.

"Sounds good to me," she said, pushing her skirt down again.

"Vroom, vroom, vroom!" The airplane flew in, bombed Max and me, and then sped out the room for a re-load.

Max reached into his faux-leather briefcase, identical to the one given to all trainees like me. Each one contained a copy of the marketing research statement (carefully prepared words to win over the customer), some legal forms (required for the placement of the free twenty volumes), and a sample volume (something to show the product's quality).

"Believe me, you won't regret it. I mean, a free set of encyclopedias! I don't know how the company does it." Max shook his head reflecting his disbelief at such an incredulous deal. "Now, I'll need a little information from you." Max pulled out a form.

I half listened as Max, leaning over the coffee table he'd cleared into his desk, filled in the form as the couple gave the information requested. I looked around the small living room, spare of furniture, spotted carpet and nothing but sparse, cheap decorations. I saw no books or magazines, only a copy of TV Guide next to the rabbit-ear antenna on top of the small television set. From a large framed photo on a table near my chair, the eyes of the couple captured in their wedding attire queried me. No matter which way I looked at the picture, their eyes would not let go of me. What did they want?

The form completed, Max handed it and a pen to the husband. "Now, as I said, all you're required to do is buy each yearly supplement at $39.95 each. What we're asking you to do, since we are giving you the entire set," Max emphasized the giving part, "is that you pay for the next ten years of supplemental volumes within a period of the next twelve months. That's our way of making sure the volumes will be kept up to date. You can pay the full amount now, or monthly at a slight interest rate."

The husband and wife looked at each other. They caught the marketing catch.

Max, not oblivious to the look, was prepared. "Oh, I almost forgot to tell you. If you sign now, you'll also receive a free bookcase with the shipment."

The husband started to say something when the airplane, wings down, propelled into the room yelling, "I'm hungry. I want dinner now." Then the two-year-old, not to be ignored, started screaming and scratching when the mother fought against having her nose pulled.

A bit surprised, I heard myself say, "Maybe we should come back and finish this after dinner." I didn't look at Max, but could feel the sting of my supervisor's eyes.

The husband stood up, looking relieved. "Yeah, good idea. Let's do that. We need to get these kids settled so I can think."

"Ah, why, sure, but if you could just sign this now, every thing's filled out, that would conclude our business and then I'd not have to bother you later." Max held out the forms and a pen to the husband who pretended not to see as he picked up his son.

The two-year-old began screaming, "Mommy mean! Mommy mean!" The airplane kept repeating he needed fuel.

"Come back about seven," the husband said over the screams, and then I swear he smiled at me.

In stone-faced silence, Max put everything back in his important-looking briefcase.

Once outside, he let loose on me. "Why the hell did you do that? I had them ready to sign, had 'em cold. You killed the sale, you know that? I was on a roll today."

I started to say, "Sale? Don't you mean placement?" Instead, I tried to sound blameless. "You can sign them after dinner. The husband said to come back at seven."

"No way! They won't be home. If they are, they'll hide in the dark and pretend. I know! I can't believe you did that! You do that on your own tomorrow, you'll never make a sale," the supervisor warned me, veins in his forehead ready to pop.

The next evening, Max, not over yesterday's loss, dropped me off in my assigned territory, half-heartedly wished me luck on my own, and told me he would pick me up at six-thirty for a dinner break at a designated corner. Company rules required territorial supervisors to drop off and pick up their newly assigned personnel.

I walked for two or three blocks along a row of 1950-style tract houses, ringing doorbells or knocking on a few doors. At two places, people did answer, but expressed no interest. Most doors never opened, and I felt a growing relief when there was no response.

I smiled as I thought about the young family that hadn't been home when we went back last night. As expected, Max had given me the "I-told-you-so speech." As contrite as possible, I had assured Max I'd learned a valuable lesson in market research.

And I had.

Spotting a bus-stop bench near my pickup spot, I sat down, took my sample Volume VII from my important looking briefcase, and found the section on Icarus. I had plenty of time. Max wouldn't be picking me up for another two hours.

The letter read like this:

October 8, 1968

Dear Son,

What I feared most about your moving to California has happened. You've become a Communist. I can't believe a son of mine could turn his back on his country, especially since you volunteered to serve your country in the navy. It pains me to say this, but I must write you out of my life.

Good-bye from a broken-hearted father.

Wait! What?

At first, I gave a nervous laugh, thinking maybe this was an over-dramatic joke. I looked more closely at the handwriting. Definitely my dad's. We'd been writing back and forth for years. What's got into him?

I read the letter again.

Me, a communist? Writing me off as his son? What was he talking about?

I'd been living and teaching in California for ten years. Now, all of a sudden, that makes me a Communist?

Was he serious? What was going on with my father?

This was not the father I knew. My mind ran wild with instances of the father I did know. The father who took his young son on trips to his relatives in the South so the boy could experience first-hand the harm of racism. The father who became a board member of the church our family attended when I told him my Sunday school teacher taught us dancing is a sin. The patient father who taught me how to drive, and surprised me with understanding after my first automobile accident. Could the writer of this letter be the man who joined the Book of the Month club so there would be books in the house for me to read to broaden my outlook on life? The same man who went into debt to help pay for my college education?

What has happened, Dad?

I know I didn't always live up to your expectations. You often worked late when I was young. I know your job required it, but it did mean I saw little of you my early years. But one event stands out for me. I think it was a company picnic or get-together of some kind. I was about seven or eight. A ball game made up of father-son teams was organized. When it was my turn at bat, an important run was needed for our team. I could tell you expected me to do something to save us, to make you proud, but I struck out. Disappointment covered your face, a look I remember now, and I cried making it all the worse. I've borne a type of guilt for that, even though I can qualify my actions by reminding you I never played ball before that day. Didn't own a baseball bat. Never had a father throw me a practice pitch. How could you have expected me to make you proud? I'd like to think maybe that look wasn't just about me.

But that's a big minor in our lives.

Remember, Dad, what was I? Ten? I was scooting around on the concrete basement floor with one foot on the back of my little brother's tricycle when I rammed into the basement door. The glass half of the door shattered and a large hunk dropped loose and stabbed me in the wrist. I don't remember it hurting much at first, just the wonder of the changing dark patterns splattered on the concrete floor as my blood gushed and spurted from my wrist. I knew from other cuts and scrapes that Mom would want to put iodine on the cut, so I didn't want to go upstairs and show her.

But you heard the noise from the crash and called down, "What happened? What are you doing down there?"

I didn't answer. I felt mesmerized by the flood of dark red leaving me. I felt nothing of my slashed wrist, only that I wanted no iodine.

"Son, what's going on? Answer me!"

When I didn't, you came part way down the stairs and saw me holding out a leaking arm.

"Oh, my god! What have you done?"

You came all the way down and had me sit on a step while you examined my wrist.

"Oh, good lord!"

After that, I don't remember much. I went lightheaded and only recall spotty moments. You must have put some kind of bandage or tourniquet on me; I don't remember. I do remember you had to carry me up a long, narrow flight of stairs to a doctor's office. God, that must have been a strain. I was stitched up and told I should be thankful you, Dad, had been swift and saved me from more blood loss, and that the ligament to my thumb had been saved. I also remember you had to carry me down those stairs and eventually to my bed, where I was ordered to stay for three weeks while I recovered from blood loss.

At least I avoided the iodine.

The next day, when you came home, you brought me a couple of comic books to read and set our only radio next to my bed for my entertainment. When I said I was sorry about breaking the door window and not telling you right away, he scoffed. "Ah, don't worry about it. Just thankful you're going to be okay now." Then you added, "Don't be so afraid of iodine next time, okay?"

Dad, look. You can still see the scar on my wrist.

I know you had my interests at heart. Remember those lace-up boots I wanted, the kind that lumberjacks wore? How I wanted those! But so impractical, as Mom pointed out. I'd out grow them before the heels wore down. And costly—more than two good pairs of shoes. But as I remember, you won a contest at work by signing on more new clients than anyone else. You used the prize money to buy those boots for me when it could have been used to pay off some of your monetary debts.

And I'll never forget the time I pretended I'd found a fifty-cent piece on the sidewalk. It was right after my cousin Patsy had visited and had lost hers. I did find it where I said I did, but I knew and you knew it belonged to her. When you confronted me, god, how ashamed and embarrassed I felt. But you reprimanded me without anger, more by explaining your disappointment in my lack of honesty, and how I should come to you if I needed money or anything. It was more than a lesson in humility.

Then there was the time I came home from junior high school with a very sore tailbone. Our one-armed PE teacher ruled with a smoothed oak paddle with holes drilled in it so that it made a whistling sound just before making contact. If our class did anything out of line, we got to meet his paddle. I don't remember what I did wrong, but that day I bent over as directed and heard the wind passing through the holes in the paddle just before it struck. He aimed too high and, oh, I received more than a message.

When I told you what happened, you came to my PE class the next day and spoke with my instructor.

"What did he say?" I asked when we were home, worried that he told you I deserved the paddle for whatever it was I no longer remember I did.

"It's not what he said. It's what I said," you answered.

"What?" I wasn't sure I wanted to hear.

"I told him if he ever hit you with that paddle again, I would personally show him what it felt like."

The teacher never used that paddle in my class again.

I have to say, Dad, your letter has hit me harder than that paddle ever did.

And remember when I had that newspaper route? What was I, thirteen or so? True, it didn't last long, because you saw me struggling with it. The winter months were severe, and you saw me battling my way through the cold wind or deep snow, trying to keep my papers dry. I had trouble collecting from people, some hiding from me when I came to collect. Enough, you said. Quit. You've proved yourself. You don't know how happy I was at those words.

You and Mom get high marks for the way you provided my introduction into the teenage mystery of sex. I was down in the basement shoveling coal into the furnace and noticed an open book on a table. Why was the book there? It never had been before. It was a nurse's handbook. I couldn't believe what I was seeing: pictures of a woman's private parts in various stages of giving birth. I don't know how long I stayed down there reading and looking at pictures of the female anatomy and drawings of sexual intercourse. It dawned on me that you had put the book there for me. Did you do it because you were too embarrassed to bring up the subject, or was I not asking you the right questions? I didn't know what I should do. Leave the book there or take it up to my room? I left it there, checking to see every day if it was still there. One day it was gone and no mention of it was ever made.

Well done.

You were proud of me when I turned sixteen and landed a job working after school at Tri-City Grocery. I gave you part of my pay every week to help with household expenses. You wanted me to learn responsibility and the value of money. It wasn't until after I graduated that you told me you had put the money aside for my college education.

We never really talked about my attending college. I wasn't much interested in school. I never applied anywhere. Why should I? I had a job, a girlfriend, the use of your car when you came home from work. I was content. But you surprised me. One day you told me you had talked to the principal of my high school and found that I was eligible for a scholarship to Southern Illinois University. That's when you told me the money I had given you was for college use. You and Mom had never discussed college attendance with me. Neither of you had gone to college, but suddenly you insisted I should take advantage of the scholarship.

And so I did. And it was one of the best things that ever happened to me. I entered a world I never knew existed. I became excited about learning for the first time I could remember. You are responsible for that. Did I ever thank you?

But after a year and a half, the draft board had my number, and I was about to be called to the army. So I joined the navy. You were proud of me for enlisting, but worried I might never finish college. I promised you that I would. And I did.

I remember after graduating Navy boot camp, I spent about two weeks in misery because all of my buddies got their duty orders, but I didn't because of some clerical foul-up. I was left at boot camp knowing no one, doing the odd shit details, having no idea when my orders would come in. I wrote home expressing my misery and wishing I'd never joined the Navy. Ironically, when my orders did come, I was sent to Los Alamitos Naval Air Station, at that time the playground of the Navy. I fell into a "hog heaven job," as you would say.

I was called into the Chaplain's office one day and asked why I was so unhappy in the Navy. I had no idea what he meant. Unknown to me, you had written to the Bureau of Naval Personnel after getting my letter from boot camp telling them how unhappy I was. The Bureau contacted the Chaplain at the naval base to check up on me. Once I explained to the Chaplain the background of the letter, we had a good laugh. I couldn't believe you were so disturbed on my behalf that you would write a letter to the Navy sharing my misery. While I was embarrassed as well as appreciative that you were looking out for me, I should have seen then that I needed to be more careful about what I said in letters to you.

I'm really sorry I didn't listen to you when I announced I was getting married. I had that twenty-one-year-old attitude that held I knew what was best for me. I'd only known the girl/woman for seven weeks and thought I was in love. Unfortunately, the navy was about to transfer me to a ship on the East coast and I impetuously got married. You gave me good reasons not to do it: away from home, lonely, infatuated, no need for the rush, she could wait until I came back, you'll never finish college...

You were right about everything but my not finishing college. I did, and my efforts had much to do with doing it for you. I gave that marriage my best shot. But on that front, you were right.

I searched your letter again, looking for some clue as to why you had written me off, but saw nothing.

So I called mom.

"Mom, I just got Dad's letter. What's going on?"

When she heard my voice it took her a minute to stop her sobbing. "I...I'm never going to get to see my grandchildren again. I just know it. This is just...just awful." More sobs.

"Mom, I don't understand. What's got into Dad? I'm confused. What does he mean he's writing me off as a son?"

"Something you said in your last letter upset him."

"My letter?" I couldn't begin to imagine what I said that would set him off.

"Yes. Something you wrote…" she sniffled… "made him feel you had become…" she sounded as if she couldn't catch a breath, her voice dropped, "… anti-American…a communist."

"A communist. My god. Is he there? I need to talk to him."

"No, he's at work."

"Should I call him there?"

She sigh-sobbed. "I don't think… that's probably not a good idea."

"That bad, huh?" Then I asked, "Mom, you don't think I've turned communist, do you? I mean, I can't think of anything I said that would even imply that."

"Well, it was that part about your students that got him upset the most."

"What did I say? Can you read that part to me?"

She went to get the letter and sounded calmer when she got back on the line.

"Here," she said. "I think it was this part." She began reading my letter:

> I had a nice visit from some of my former students who are now at UC Berkeley. They had participated in one of the protests going on against the Vietnam War, even placing themselves in danger when the police threatened with tear gas and batons. They posed some solid arguments and reasoning to back up their positions. They jarred me loose from my superficial acceptance of what was going on. Having been raised through World War II and participating in the Korean War, I thoughtlessly accepted what was going on in Vietnam and just went about my business of teaching. I couldn't help but liken those students to Huck Finn, who was willing to go against the established thinking of the time and even go to hell rather than turn Jim in to the authorities. They were willing to go the distance against the establishment for what they believed in.

She stopped reading.

"That's it?" I asked. "That makes me a communist? I don't get it."

"Well, we see a lot of those student protests on television, you know. They act ugly and don't seem to appreciate the country they live in. And, you know, the way they dress, the long hair and all. All that yelling and protesting."

Ah, I understood now and realized I had to be careful how I responded to her comments. She was partly on my dad's side.

"Look, Mom. I'm not a communist and I'm not a hippie. All I was trying to say in that letter was that my students were willing to go the limit to share their beliefs and expose what to them is wrong with the Vietnam policies. Because I admire them for that does not make me a communist. What they have done is shake me from my lethargy and cause me to pay more attention to what our objectives are in Vietnam. Does Dad know what those objectives are? Do you know? Ask yourself, is it better to just go along with what is, or question what is? Which is being a better citizen? Dad has always said there are three sides to every story: your side, my side and the right side. Remind him of that. Tell him I called, that he is wrong labeling me a communist for what I wrote. And I hope you're convinced. Tell him I'll wait to hear from him. That's all I can do."

Almost two disquieting weeks went by before I heard from my father again in a very brief letter saying my mother explained everything, and that they planned to come visit at Christmas if it was all right. No words of regret or apology or of politics. But the damage had been done. My letters home became less frequent and very short, restricted mostly to how the family was doing.

My parents did come visit at Christmas, and no mention of my letter or politics was raised. They came and left as if nothing untoward had ever transpired. For me, holiday cheer felt more lackluster from previous years. I realized later that my dad and I managed knowingly or not to avoid being alone in the same room. Did he feel toward me the tension and caution I felt around him while he visited? Did he still think I was a Communist but was avoiding confrontation? Had his feelings toward me changed? Should I have said something?

I'll never know.

I only know he left behind a son whose broken-heart still hasn't healed.

Thirteen years ago, I was involved in an unpleasant incident that in the scheme of things was nothing much. Yet, as the protagonist says in Beckett's novel *Malone Dies*, "Nothing is more real than nothing," and so the feelings roused in me by the incident continue to itch away at me like a rash for which there is no adequate cure, and I cannot seem to reconcile my disappointment with reality.

Back then, my wife and I, along with our then seventeen-year-old daughter and her friend, were on our way to Los Angeles for a weekend get-a-way we'd been planning for weeks: rooms at the Omni Hotel, dinner reservations at the Water Grill, tickets for an Audra McDonald concert at the recently opened Disney Music Center, and then maybe the LACMA, if we could convince the girls. Our moods were high with anticipation and the car filled with the girls' happy chatter about getting to see one of their favorite singers in the much talked about Frank Gehry music hall.

Before leaving town, I stopped at an Exxon service station to fill up. As I pulled in from the street, I noticed an old, faded yellow Mustang, a '60s vintage, I think, starting to back out of the station, but it stopped when it saw me turning in.

I pulled up to one of the gas pumps, got out, and slid my credit card into the slot, followed the routine directions, and started filling the tank when a man got out of the Mustang and in a truculent voice yelled, "Hey, asshole! You! You almost hit me!"

Thrown for the moment, I just looked at him, not relating yet to what he was talking about. "You yelling at me?"

He continued toward me, pointing his finger like a weapon. Unshaven, he looked to be in his mid '30s, husky build, slightly curly sandy hair, and a fierce look on his face. "Don't play dumb, dick-head. You pulled in not looking and almost hit me as I was backing away from the air pump. You realize how close you came to hitting my car? You came this close when you pulled in." He gestured a small space between his thumb and forefinger. "You in such a hurry you can't watch where you're going?"

His face showed such outrage over what I considered a nonevent that I almost found it humorous. "But I didn't hit you," I said. "Maybe you should be more careful when you back up into on-coming traffic. Anyway, no damage has been done. So what's the problem?"

He moved too close to me, putting his face in mine. "You! You're my problem." I noticed spittle in the corners of his mouth. Mad dog, I thought.

I took a step back, no longer feeling any humor. "Look, you were backing up when I was pulling in. You were moving into the flow of traffic. You did what you should have done, so what's the fuss?"

He took a step forward again and snarled, "I want an apology, asshole."

"For what?" Then I said what I shouldn't have. "Seems to me you're being the asshole here."

"Wha'd you call me?" He said it like a warning, but I was too slow to pick up on the fact he wanted me to provoke him. His mouth formed a grin.

"You heard me," I said.

The pump handle clicked, letting me know the tank was full. I'd had enough of this ludicrous encounter and wanted to get on with the family plans. I started to turn from my accuser to put the pump handle back into the pump slot when he shoved me hard in the chest with both hands, knocking me off balance and against the gas pump, the hose and nozzle hitting the ground. My knees buckled and I almost went down but caught myself.

Now my wife was out of the car, screaming my name and coming to my aid, and the girls, who had not been paying much attention, were trying to understand what was happening, asking what was the matter. Their voices became noise mixed in with the odor of gasoline.

Stunned, I regained partial balance, but as I looked into the face of my attacker, time held still long enough to envelope my past, present and future all in the same instant. Part of me slipped out of the present, feeling again the anger that I had experienced when I was at Boy Scout camp and gave Tyler a bloody nose for continually calling me "Four Eyes" because I wore glasses. That moment of aggression on my part ironically turned me into a camp hero of sorts. Praised for standing up to a bully and bloodying his nose, I was rewarded for my violent behavior by being selected for the Order of the Arrow. Maybe my attacker was simply a karmic Tyler getting even with me.

Simultaneously, in this exact time-warped moment, I saw me hit back at this crazy person. It didn't matter that he was twenty years younger and could easily beat me. I went after him regardless. Don't let him get away with hitting you. Don't take this sick man's guff. So, take a cut face, maybe a broken tooth. So what? He should be put down. Hit the bully back. Keep hitting him.

Time snapped back to the present, and I hadn't moved. I still stood there by the gas pump, Tyler fading away, hearing someone say, "Don't hit him."

At first I thought my mind was speaking to me. But the voice came from a young man standing on the other side of the gas pump. He stood by a red, R J Carroll Plumbing truck. He wasn't looking at me, but at the man who had pushed me.

My attacker said, "Did you see what he did?" He pointed at me. "He almost hit my car."

"I don't know what he did, and I don't care," the young man said. "Just don't hit him again."

"This a-hole came speeding in here and almost hit my car," he whined, not wanting to give up.

"No, I didn't see that. I'm just saying, don't him again."

"But he almost hit me!" His anger flared up and he stared at me, hate emanating from his eyes, fists opening and closing, wanting so much for blood.

"But he didn't," the young man said evenly.

Red faced, the angry man looked at me, then at the intruder, then uttered a curse word or two and walked back to his car. He turned halfway back, making sure to get the last word. "Lady, teach your cowardly husband how to drive."

Numb and stupefied by what could have but didn't happen, I put the nozzle back in the pump, screwed the gas cap back on the car tank and looked over at the young man who had just saved me from a nasty encounter and nodded toward him. He smiled, nodded back, got in his truck and drove away before my wits returned and I could thank him.

I got in the car and my wife asked, "Are you okay?"

"Fine," I said, hiding the lie.

"Did he hurt you?" my daughter asked.

I assured them I was not hurt and, as calmly as I could, drove off saying something like it was time to get the show on the road.

"I can't believe what happened," my wife said. "That man is insane. He wanted you to fight him. Over nothing! Thank heaven you didn't let him goad you into doing something stupid."

I couldn't say what I was thinking.

"Thank goodness that young man spoke up," my wife said. "I wish he hadn't driven away so fast. I wanted to thank him."

"How can you be so calm?" my daughter asked. "I was scared he was going to hurt you."

"Nothing happened," I said. "It's over and nothing happened. Let's just forget it and enjoy the day."

But something had happened. Foolish as it was, I had wanted to fight back. I felt it in the moment. It was what he wanted me to do and what I wanted to do, despite what would have been the obvious consequences. I wanted to believe I may have struck back if that young man, a man I can't even describe anymore, hadn't interfered. And I know the outcome if I had.

So why am I haunted by this particular event, this moment frozen in time, refusing to thaw and melt into the vast lake of many other memories and be thankful it turned out as it did? Is it humiliation because I hadn't shown my family a tough man of the house, someone capable of protecting them? Was it really the young man's speaking up that kept me from retaliating, or was I afraid? Had my age turned me into the coward my accuser said I was? Or, have I not yet grown beyond some primordial flaw in human evolution?

I ask myself, especially when I see a red R J Carroll Plumbing truck, did that young man really do me a favor by interfering?

Of course.

So why am I still obsessed by it?

"See?" Stacy pointed down the hill. "Civilization. We made it." Harry knew she was trying to sound amiable, but he wasn't ready to forgive. Anger had kept him silent during the long walk back. Deliberately ignoring her, he looked down, licked his dry lips at the welcomed sight of bars and cafes curving around the crowded Cassis waterfront, ready to collapse at the nearest one.

"I'm cotton dry," Stacy continued. "And I know you're ready for a drink. Which place looks good?"

"You mean I have a choice?" Harry made certain his irritation showed.

Stacy gave him that how-do-I-put-up-with-you look he hated, then suggested, "Let's go around to the sunny side."

Hot and sticky, Harry preferred the shady side, but not certain why, he answered with an exaggerated bow and a slow sweep of his sunburned arms indicating Stacy should lead the way.

The hike back to town hadn't slowed her down like it had him. That irked him, too. Following along, he watched Stacy's sleek calf muscles show their strength with every step and couldn't help admiring the smooth, firm backs of her thighs, now sunned darker than her light tan shorts. She still walked with that confidence he had always admired, head up, back straight, arms swinging gracefully, looking assured, a little sassy. Her white blouse was damp between her shoulder blades, and her short, blonde ponytail barely covered the back of her neck. He knew the body, the pleasure he found hidden beneath those clothes.

An attractive forty-year-old, Stacy still made men's heads turn and that always made him proud. But right now, he wished his wife would just keep walking and disappear into the crowd. No, maybe that's what *he* should do, just vanish into the unknown, some place where he could better accept his present position.

Argumentative most of the day, he'd disagreed on everything from where to park the car that morning to which boat tour to take to the *calanques*. He had wanted to take the round trip that took in all three coves near Marseilles, but when the young man in the French tourist office suggested they get off the boat at En Vau Inlet and walk back to Cassis along a high trail, Stacy got excited and thought it would be more "adventurous." Well, she could take her "adventurous" and stick it.

What they hadn't been told was *how* you get to the high ridge trail back to town. With his slight acrophobia, that unanticipated long scramble up the steep, rocky limestone cliff to the so-called trail had been a god-awful nightmare. Every time they'd lost the white and red trail markers he felt his anger toward Stacy magnify, every slip and scratch became her fault.

His only pleasure had come from looking down at the occasional fear in her eyes when his footing would slip and loosened rocks would cascade down her way.

"Happy now?" he had yelled at one point. "Enjoying this?" Once they'd reached the path at the top, he hadn't said another word all the way back.

Reliving it now only fed his anger at Stacy. Himself. They weren't prepared for such an encounter. The wrong shoes, no water, no trail map. Hell, four long, hot hours just to get back to town when all he'd wanted was a pleasant little boat trip to view the Mediterranean coastline, not climb it. She was so much better at accepting the unexpected, while he let things fester into irritability, making him all the more upset at her...him...oh, hell.

Well, they were back. He should let it all go.

But it wasn't that easy. What made him give in to her so much? Like just now, why hadn't he said he wanted to sit on the shady side?

Why did he go along with her so much and then become angry with her, then himself? What was wrong with him, anyway? He was a damn accommodation junkie, that's what he was. Rationally, he knew his anger was more with himself than with Stacy, but she made an easier target.

Even this, his first and maybe only sabbatical leave he'd ever be able to afford, wasn't turning out well, although admittedly he didn't know what he had expected. After fourteen years of waiting, didn't he deserve something new, different, rewarding? God knows he desperately needed this break from teaching history to high school kids who seemed to get rowdier and more difficult every year. Fewer and fewer seemed to want to learn. Half his time he spent disciplining or confiscating cell phones. Their parents didn't seem to care, either. No one who didn't teach could know the strain and stress.

But while he really hadn't envisioned anything in particular after finishing up his sabbatical project other than an escape from the norm, he expected *something* to change for the better. He hoped for—no, *needed*—some rejuvenating transformation in his life.

But what?

As he followed Stacy through the maze of other tourists, Harry tried to convince himself to relax, drop it all. Only two weeks left before returning home. You're in Cassis, a lovely place this time of year. A million other people would be glad to trade places with you. Shake yourself loose. Be glad for what you have. Look around you.

Despite the rows of stores hawking the usual tourist potpourri, Harry liked the way the buildings receded into the hills behind. He could see why artists were attracted to the area. Admiring the neat rows of small, colorful boats tied up around the harbor, he almost plowed into Stacy, who had stopped at a noisy, busy café bar around the bend on *Quai Calendal*. A huge, red awning stretched out over red captain chairs scattered around small tables covered with red cloths. He didn't see an empty table.

He would have picked a quieter place, but Stacy had this thing about crowded markets, restaurants and cafés, certain they must be better or so many people wouldn't be there. He had suggested once that maybe people are like lemmings. She hadn't bought his analogy. Look who's the little lemming today, he reminded himself.

Harry trailed Stacy as they made their way to a table surrounded by the pleasant sounds of French. He wished he understood and spoke the language better. They had taken a French class a couple of nights a week in preparation for this trip, but it hadn't done him much good. She picked the language up quickly, getting even better since their arrival four weeks ago. Good enough, anyway, to constantly correct him when he misused or misinterpreted certain phrases.

Stacy relaxed into her chair. "God! I'm really parched. What're you going to have?"

He didn't want to share how good it felt to sit. What he wanted was cold water but what came out was, "A kir." He tried to imply in his tone, "Naturally; what else?" He'd only recently discovered the drink and not only liked the taste, but the fact he could order one and be understood.

"A kir? Not very thirst quenching. I'm for beer. You don't want a beer?"

She was right, of course. A kir was not going to quell his thirst.

"I want a kir. Maybe two, maybe even three." He noticed she started to say something but then let it pass.

They remained silent watching the crowds pass until the waiter finally came for their order. As clearly as he could, he asked for *un kir et une biere* just as he had practiced it in his head. The waiter looked blank at him, then at Stacy, so she repeated their order. The waiter nodded and left.

Harry felt his jaw muscles twitch as he wished his fingers could be squeezed around the waiter's neck and Stacy's at the same time.

When their drinks came, Stacy gave a polite *merci* to the waiter, but Harry ignored his presence with as much distain as he could show, though he knew the waiter didn't give a shit.

As they sat in silence, two attractive couples, dressed in leisurely affluence, made their way to a nearby table. The blond with doe-like eyes and a tan he thought she probably worked on all year, leaned toward him, smiled, and asked something in French. He caught her perfume but not her words. Too slowly, he grasped that she wanted to use one of the empty chairs at his table. He half stood, nearly knocking over his own chair, fumbling with, "*Mais, certainment,*" and began a pliant nodding. His face flushed with an angry awareness of himself.

The woman took the chair back to her table, but the disturbing trace of her presence stayed, bringing on that rueful uneasiness that frequently caught him off guard and rushed over him, leaving him powerless to stop the unwanted feelings. Just the mere sight of her did it again—that dreaded, resentful dissatisfaction he experienced too often surfaced.

Harry stared at the lively foursome, at the woman. Only a table away, but worlds apart, their world, her world, her. Resentment at who she was, what she just did to him, moved in like an unwelcomed storm. Looking at her made him embarrassed, melancholy, anxious, provoked, envious—all entangled in some sort of sexuality. Yes, there was that, yes. A female power, a male envy? No, it was more, much more. She...be honest...*they*...women like her...always symbolized some missed life, some longing, some flaw in him, like an infection of displeasure.

Was that all it was? Displeasure with his own life? A dormant desire for an essence of life now lost? No, never lost, no, because he knew women like her represented what could never be obtained by someone like himself, a high school teacher. He knew what social status was appropriated to teachers: *those who can do, those who can't...*

Look away, blink away those unsettling thoughts.

But Harry's eyes couldn't let go of the woman, his thoughts weaving oblong blurs, wondering what life with her would be like, what sex would be like with her....

"So, you like that."

Stacy jarred him back to his own table.

"What? Sorry?" He tried to feign innocence. Her hurt showed, making him feel even worse, yet inwardly content she looked unhappy.

"Oh, god, just forget it." She turned away.

He let her think she understood his disproportionate thoughts. But how could she when he didn't really understand himself?

Or did he?

Feeling bewitched, he looked again at the woman at the other table, uncomfortably remembering the bittersweet moment he'd first encountered this feeling, first felt like this—years ago—his after-school job at the supermarket—the produce department—stacking a display of oranges…

She had come in with her father. Harry's adolescent eyes immediately understood these were people who mattered to the world. Their white tennis outfits accentuated their tans, their elegance, their rich distance. No one he knew even owned a tennis racket, let alone played. She was probably seventeen, his age, and he'd never seen any one more desirable, more emblematic of what he wasn't. What was it he was seeing he'd never noticed before?

Embarrassed even now, he remembered his astonishment at his urge to run his tongue along her bare arms and legs colored light caramel by the sun, so smooth and wholesome sleek. Her long, brown hair, bleached blond in spots from the sun, had been tied back with a violet-blue ribbon the color of her eyes, every feature of her face revealing perfection, blinding him from comprehending the words she spoke. Her light voice, an unfamiliar melody, played counterpoint against her handsome father's deep voice as they examined and discussed the produce. At once, Harry-the-grocery-clerk wanted what they were, to step into their lives, to be one of them.

Then she came over to him asking something about the oranges. With no understanding, he feared looking for very long into her clear, violet eyes and stammered some obtuse sounding answer, dropped an orange at her perfect feet, bent down to pick it up, never wanting to rise, only to look forever at her clean, white tennis shoes, her long, firm, smooth brown legs. Oh, just to touch them!

The very fabric of his life ripped open in that moment and spilled obeisance at her feet. When he dared look up into her laughing face again, he knew in that moment a life existed to which he could never belong. She was untouchable, unreachable. She didn't know it, but she had passed sentence on him. After all these years, he still remembered that moment…her…

"Sometimes you're a real asshole, Harry."

"Sorry, what'd you say?" This time Harry truly hadn't heard Stacy.

"I said you're a bore and embarrassing me the way you're staring at those people. I want to go. You win the silence contest, okay? I want to eat and go back to the hotel." Stacy stood up abruptly, not waiting for an answer.

"Yeah, sure. Fine." A great sigh escaped him, as though he'd been holding his breath for a day. His red face felt hot, but not from the day's sun. His first thought, let her go back alone. He'd stay, have another drink. She knew her way.

Stacy wove her way through the crowded tables and chairs, leaving Harry to pay the check. By the time he'd gotten the waiter's attention, clarified the euros and paid, she was nearly halfway around the quay where she had stopped, not looking back, and waited in front of the Hotel Liautaud.

When he got to her, she told him, "I'd like to eat here. One of the travel books says the restaurant upstairs has great bouillabaisse."

He hated bouillabaisse, and she knew it. Well, she was angry and no doubt this was meant to punish him. He started to put up an argument, to remind her he didn't care much for fishy foods, but he found himself feeling guilty, like it must feel to be caught having an affair, though his lusts were mostly in his head.

"Fine." But to gain some control he added, "Just don't ask me to share." Stacy had this thing about sharing what they ordered, especially desserts.

"The mood you're in, I wouldn't ask you for a thing."

He couldn't think of a clever retort, so followed Stacy up the stairs to the restaurant where every table had a perfect view of the harbor. The thick linen napkins folded like spread-open accordions fanned out in front of the tall-stemmed crystal goblets. Too many pieces of silverware gleamed on either side of large silver plates. The stoic *maitre de*, dressed in black stuffiness, and numerous waiters standing around in their white linen jackets, black bow ties, the clichéd napkin across one arm, scrutinized their entrance. By French standards they were too early for dinner, the only ones in the restaurant.

At once, Harry felt out of place and wanted to leave. The two of them were dusty and sweaty from their hiking. He wanted to shower, to change clothes, just grab a pizza. As they were led to a table, he felt the *maitre de* had them pegged as little worthy of his attention, sensed his disrespect, irritating Harry all the more.

After they sat, each was rather elaborately handed a huge, leather-covered, two-pound menu, as they were wished "*Bon appetit*" with a smile that lasted barely a second. Teeth grating, cheeks flushed, Harry wished for the nerve to hit Stacy with the menu.

The cheapest item on all twelve pages was euros ridiculous and that was *a la carte*. The renowned bouillabaisse dinner was euros outrageous.

"Are you sure you won't share with me? I didn't expect these prices." Stacy's tone was decidedly friendlier as she peeked meekly around the tall menu, giving him a slight flush of satisfaction.

Harry took his time looking through the menu again before he answered. "I'm really not hungry. I could do with just a green salad."

"Well, would you at least have a little if I order it? It's so expensive."

You wanted bouillabaisse, now you eat it.

"You know I don't like the stuff. It's too fishy tasting." He enjoyed his determination not to give in to her this time.

"Yes, but you've never had really good bouillabaisse. This place is known for it. You might like it the way they do it here."

He kept looking at the menu, silent.

"Why are you always afraid to try anything new?"

Her words struck some cord of recognition he didn't want to hear. His look must have softened her.

"Look, I'm sorry. I didn't know it would be like this. Would you rather go? You look uncomfortable. We can still leave."

She was offering him an out with an apology, something he felt he deserved, but the idea of getting up now, after drinking the water that had just been poured, after seeing the prices on the menu, after remembering the looks they got when they came in, after what she had just said, he'd be damned if he'd be further humiliated by leaving.

"No, no," he said with a pseudo graciousness she misunderstood. "You go ahead and get the bouillabaisse. I'll order a dinner salad. We'll just order the house wine."

"Sure?"

"Yeah, sure."

He saw this relieved Stacy. She sat back and looked out the window.

"So pretty, isn't it, the way the ebbing light casts rainbow reflections on the water?"

"Mm."

But he saw something reflected in the window she didn't—himself. What did that forty-three-year-old face reveal? What did that face want?

The *garçon* approached and caught Harry off guard. Stacy looked at Harry but he said nothing, so she began a playful conversation in a mixture of French and English with the waiter, asking questions about the menu, the bouillabaisse, what was in it, what size portions were in an order, and what good cheap wine he'd recommend. He flinched when she asked for a cheap wine even though that's what they could afford.

Harry noticed the waiter enjoyed conversing with Stacy, carrying on an innocent flirtation. Did this Frenchman find her attractive? She looked so alive and appealing that he wanted to reach across the table and kiss the long, smooth curve of her neck while she was looking up at the waiter. He suppressed an urge to touch the little smile wrinkles around her eyes. He enjoyed the way she laughed at herself when the waiter teased about a mispronounced word. She seemed so satisfied with who she was.

Watching her interaction with the waiter, Harry found he wanted to relive their day, yes, to really live it this time, to delight in their hot hike, to relish overcoming the dangerous climb, to take pleasure in sitting on the quay drinking cold beer together, to appreciate being in France away from teaching. Why hadn't he done that? Why did he now want what he could have had? Why did he long for what he couldn't have? Why wasn't there a switch he could just turn?

Harry realized the waiter had left and Stacy was trying to make things right, apologizing for her part in a tense day, sorry about their silly arguing. Couldn't they enjoy the rest of the day?

She loved him, he realized. And at that moment, he knew he loved her.

He started to say she'd been fine, that it was all his fault, when the attractive foursome he'd seen earlier came into the restaurant. A sad thrill jolted him when the other woman glanced his way, gave what he thought might be a slight smile. Would she have remembered him? Then the woman fell into animated conversation and laughter with her companions. With anguished uncertainty, Harry wondered if their sniggers had to do with his earlier foolish reaction to her at the café. Did she remember his awkwardness over the chair? Were they laughing at the silly American?

He instantly sank into that place he hated, that uncomfortable place those people always took him—like that summer math seminar in Santa Barbara—at a fiesta parade, his zoom lens happened to catch her face on the other side of the street, shutting out everything else. She sat with the prestigious people in a box decorated in red, white, and green above the crowd. Her face suggested boredom. For several minutes he kept her in focus, secretly watching her, unaware of the numerous camera clicks. The shiniest, blackest hair he had ever seen. Spanish features, her olive skin, baby smooth, as if it had no pores.

Her intense black eyes had surprised him, caught him, stared back at him, right through his camera lens into his being. For an endless moment, those eyes taunted, pulled him toward some sorely craved zone, a place of rich mystery and seductiveness. They drew him, tempted, teased, mocked. Just viewing her striking features upset him, sent him again where he didn't want to go, that place he couldn't name. He craved her, hated her, wanted her beyond the sexual, beyond the physical, wanted to be in her life, wanted her life in ways he still couldn't fathom, wanted something he couldn't label, knew he couldn't have, still wanted. She was a have, he a have not. Mesmerized, the camera clicked, clicked, clicked.

But soon he lowered his camera, shutting out the light, leaving himself in continual conflict with a memory of something forever unobtainable. Later, after memorizing the pictures, he deleted them before Stacy could see them.

And there were other times.

And in those revealing, provoking moments of sad desire, a strange, almost enjoyed discontentment surfaced, drenching him with ambiguous feelings. He wanted these feelings to be math problems he could solve, equations with answers. Search as he could, he never seemed to find the right formula for solutions to his problematic desires.

———

And now the inaccessible had surfaced again, reminding him of his place in life. Wasn't it Montaigne, he mused, who said that no matter where the traveler went he could never get away from himself? Well, was he one of those who could never travel all the way into life, but instead allowed only to know of it? The life he wanted wasn't his to have. He wasn't who he wanted to be, nor could ever be.

So accept it.

Was it that simple?

In that moment, he craved obliteration of the obsessive wall that blocked him from assembling himself, leaving him with a perverse pride in knowing he was a slave to impossibility.

On the far side of the table, Stacy took his hand, said something about how lucky they were to have this time off, how fortunate they could at last afford to travel in France, how lovely the *calanques* were today, how unexpectedly steep the trail was, how she truly worried at one or two dangerous places, how they really could have slipped and fallen several hundred feet.

"But we did it. We made it, didn't we, Harry?"

He looked as if seeing her face for the first time and saw what he now realized he didn't deserve.

THE BLUE HAZE

No one can convince me they aren't out there. Just two or three blocks away, oh yes. I know it; feel it. My mind keeps seeing them sitting there in a black Ford panel truck; I see them hunched over their machines, wearing this special electronic gear they have, taping everything. Yeah. I've read about those devices. They can listen through walls, yes, maybe miles! I'll bet now they can even see through the walls. Oh, yeah, they're out there. Looking—listening—laughing—waiting…

Yes, waiting for me. Ah, wouldn't they just love to bust a college professor, stoned up his wahzoo. And with one of his students! You know they would. Of course, that's what they want. That's why they're out there, isn't it? They live for it. I'm positive. Out there looking for news the public loves to hear. Gotcha, gotcha, gotcha, Teach. Busted, busted, buddy boy. Cha, cha, cha.

"Another hit?"

Greg holds the joint out to me. Do I want another hit? Funny word—"hit."

I guess I do. But I'm not really sure. I take it from Greg who has a grin as big as Martha Rae's mouth. Is it spelled R-a-e or R-a-y? You know. That funny lady, the actress with the big mouth. Did Polident ads—or Polygrip—something like that for dentures. But

Greg doesn't need dentures, and he doesn't really have a big mouth. It just looks big from where I sit, floating, floating. Nice.

Or am I standing? No, I am sitting, I think, here in my house. Yes. We're doing some home schooling, an experiment, way long overdue. It's new to me, this getting high—stoned—whacked—buzzed—enlightened. I've held off enlightenment all these years. But I've gotten more curious over time. This is the only way to find the truth, the truth that's out there. Everybody says so. But the government denies it. Not enough studies done to prove it's not harmful. More studies, they say. So why aren't they studying it, like we are? Should I be taking notes?

They wouldn't understand, the hunched over ones out there, listening in. Oh, I'm on to you boys in blue. No, you'd have DEA stamped in big letters on your backs. You don't want what I'm doing to be legal 'cause you'd lose your jobs. Go ahead; wag your finger.

Fear jabs, escalates. "Close the drapes. They can see and hear everything." My usually authoritative teacher voice sounds mushy. Big pauses between syllables. Do I have a big mouth myself? Not a loud mouth. I mean big—physically? Size wise?

"You just closed them," Greg tells me.

"What?"

"You just closed the drapes. They're closed."

Greg, still grinning, takes the joint from me. Did I take a drag? Another funny word—"drag." I don't remember. Doesn't matter. Another of the experiment's glossary—pot, joint, stick, hit, drag, toke, kush, grass, busted.

Busted. Yuck! Such a hard sound. Bust-ed.

"College professor and his student arrested in drug bust! That's tomorrow's headlines," I tell Greg 'cause I just know they're out there, laughing, enjoying my paranoia, waiting for the right time. I should not have ignored the possibility, the possible. Almost hear them laughing…

Greg tells me I'm experiencing wasted—wasted. Hmm. Like Eliot says in *The Waste Land*, "You *are* a proper fool…" Oh. I get it now. "Too old too soon; too wise too late," yeah? I diddled my youth instead of fiddled.

I can't catch my mind, my thoughts…

"Hey, come on, man, relax." Greg sucks on the doobie, that's what he calls it, holding his breath like he showed me. Hands the joint back between thumb and index finger. "Don't be so fearful. Nobody's out there. Nothing's gonna happen. Relax. Enjoy. Enjoy your experiment."

Greg, my best student, now my teacher, my medicine man. He's sharp, this Greg. An Afghan vet, oldest one in my class. Seen some bad shit over there. Back home in one piece, though. Looks like that Italian actor, Marcello Mastroianni. Girls stare at him. He calls me The Man.

Oh, man, what's happening?

Why'd I say yes to this? 'Cause it's my idea. I told him about my body pains, bad arthritis. "Got what you need," he told me. But I kept putting him off. What made me change my mind? I'm a little dizzy. My mind keeps slipping—wants to float. Me, the man. Gather yourself.

"Wha'd you say this was?" I stare at the fat, tightly rolled paper with a long ash jutting out. Amazing how long the ash is. Yeah! Look how long that sucker is! Why hasn't it fallen off? It holds my attention. Unbelievable. "Is this Blue Dreams?"

Greg lets out his breath all at once. "No. Acapulco gold."

On my back now. I see Elvis. It's an Elvis sighting and Ann-Margret's with him. Fun in Acapulco. Movie clips dance, wiggle on my ceiling. "Been there," I tell him. "I've been to Acapulco."

"Me, too." Greg takes the thing from my hand, making sure the ash stays on. Amazing. "That's where I got this stash." Elvis leaves. Ann-Margret lingers.

"Hot," I say. I think I mean Acapulco. Maybe not.

I look at Greg as he takes a deep drag, holds his breath, puffs out his cheeks, blows smoke rings. He sees me watching, wiggles his eyebrows like Groucho. So different from in my class. So young looking. Everybody's young looking to me. He's so serious. A budding young scholar, testing the buds of gold. He found gold in Afghanistan. He's sharing the gold.

Hey! This is a serious experiment. Where can I get my own gold? I start to laugh. I don't know why I laugh, but I do. If they're out there, maybe I shouldn't be laughing. But I giggle, then

I cough out my breath, try to stop laughing, but I let out a big whatayacallit—guffaw, whatever a guffaw is—but it sounds right for the silly sounds I'm making.

What's so funny?

I don't know. This is serious.

Greg thinks something is funny. He blows out all his air like a whale and starts to laugh, pointing at me. I don't think I'm funny, but he does so I have to laugh. I can't stop. I've never laughed like this in my long life. My side starts to ache from laughing so hard. I'm on the floor in the womb position. So's Greg. I can't think, only laugh.

"Hey, coppers. Get this on tape!" I laugh and give them the finger. Don't care anymore if they're out there. Well, I do, but I don't, know what I mean? I don't.

We stop laughing. I look at Greg. This was his idea. No, don't lie. It was mine. So don't blame him. I just mean I mentioned in my office that day that I'd never tried this stuff. Surprised him. Thought I must have used by now. I guess he thought I was cool, hip. Told him, when others were listening to Hendrix or Janis I was listening to Segovia or Van Cliburn. Drugs not so out there back then. It all passed me by. He asked me if I wanted to try it sometime, can diminish pain, he said and I said yes. Body pains I have. He's a nice kid, well, he's in his late twenties. That's a kid. But not when it comes to chemical intoxication. Says he's been doing it since over there. Only way to survive what he saw, he says. And he's got access, you know? I have no idea where you get this stuff. It's not legal but will be soon, Greg says. Medical marijuana slipping in sideways. Matter of time he says. Matter and Time. Can matter and time be mixed? What would the results be? Can't fathom it. Does time matter? Getting deep here.

The knock on the door sends liquid ice through my skin and my bones freeze. It's the cops and now I know I do care. I shiver, feel an arctic breeze. God, there goes my career. I'm dead meat. It's over. Tenure doesn't cut it in this case. And so near retirement. Morals charge. Doping with a student. Dumbdumbdumb. Drum beats. My heart bangs louder than the door knocking. Now the bell rings. Oh, man, they've got it all on tape. They'll break the door down, and I'll have to pay for a new door. What a mess. Thank god Janet's out of town and doesn't have to be humiliated. When she finds out…oh, god, she'll have to bail me out. But how? She's out of town.

"It's Sherry," Greg says. He gets up—he's really tall—and goes to the door.

"NO!" I yell. I jump from the floor, surprised at my dexterity, but only for a moment because I fall down again, my frozen body now melted. This is my house; don't open the door. The words don't leave my head.

He turns and smiles a Polident Martha. He's in charge, my teacher-student.

"She's brought food, a vital component to your education," he tells me and opens the door.

I expect dark blue, battering rams, drawn guns, bulletproof vests, batons, handcuffs.

It *is* Sherry. She holds a white cake box. No guns. No uniforms behind her. I check. My heart comes back inside me.

Sherry kisses Greg on the lips. Sherry's his girlfriend. They live together. I've met her a few times at campus parties. Lovely.

"Shut the door!" I still think they could be out there, waiting to see how many people they can catch in this den of iniquity, my home. They want to make me look as awful as possible, an appalling influence on my students. Stoned with plural students reads better than singular.

"Hi," Sherry says to me. It's a coy "hi" and I imagine she feels a little awkward. She doesn't know whether to call me by my name or the man, or professor, or doctor, or mister, or dopey old fart. Or, is it me that feels awkward? Of course, I do. I should feel awkward. I should feel ridiculous. This is ridiculous. My wife's out of town, I'm having a pot party with graduate students, and the police are waiting outside to arrest me. And what would my own children say? It's after nine. Do you know where your dad is? Are my children, like Greg and Sherry, experimenting at some other teacher's house? Are they pot smokers and I don't know it?

I say hello back and see in her every woman I've ever wanted to have sex with. Maybe I've never let myself look before. I want to run my tongue along her cheeks, absolutely the woman you want to be with on a boat sailing off to anywhere, her long, blond tresses caught in the wind. She's so young looking it makes me hate that I'm oldish, never done drugs before, and doing it for the first time with a student. With students! She makes me sad, so I fall into that state.

I'm crazy—no, mad! I don't need to look in the mirror to see my double jowls, my soft middle, the hair in my ears and nose. I am Methuselah. And she's Ann-Margret come from Acapulco. I'm trying to experience what I think I missed in my twenties, when I was young like these two. Me, old goodie two-shoes. It's not working. I'm—I'm—what am I doing, for god's sake?

Why did I wait for Janet to be gone to do this? Shouldn't she be involved? Think. What are my excuses, Janet? Maybe I'll learn and I can teach you. Should I be embarrassed? What would she think of Sherry? Not what I'm thinking.

From the floor, I stare, beckon Sherry to come in, try to act straight. She raises the white cake box. "Brought a strawberry pie."

"Kitchen's there." I point. Then I remember my manners.

"Welcome. I love strawberry pie. Thanks." I try to stand up. The floor tilts. It's going to need fixing.

"I'll show her." Greg doesn't seem zonked like me. He takes the box from her, smiles, kisses her on the cheek. Oh, god.

Sherry smiles and I want her to kiss me, look at me like that. Can you believe that? As they walk to the kitchen, they're what I want to be in that moment, a tall, dark Italian actor with a confident smile, arm around a tanned, red-haired Ann-Margret…oh…sorry Janet. I love you. A lifetime of Janet envelops me.

The moment passes. A gigantic swizzle stick stirs my mind. Nothing focuses. The swirling stops on a thought.

I've made a doobie of a mistake. Why did I think I needed this? The question lingers a long time. I think it's a long time. It's a long enough time, that's for sure, because I don't think I like whatever it is I'm thinking. What am I thinking? I'm thinking I'm a poor player, strutting and fretting my last hour upon this stage, and then no more will be heard about this tale told by an idiot, full of significant nothing.

Sherry and Greg sit next to me on the floor. She leans against the divan, her skirt rises, and I see the little butterfly tattoo on the inside of her smooth, tanned thigh. I stare. She sees my wide eyes, smiles, doesn't seem to care I stare. Sherry takes a hit from a new joint. That's what they call it. I said that already, didn't I? That's what they called it in my day. When was it ever my day? Why did it take me so long to do this? How did I talk myself into this? Oh, god.

Sherry hands me the new one. I wonder what happened to the one with the long ash? I ask. Greg laughs. I take a hit like my teacher, my medicine man, showed me earlier. I hold it in. What a good student am I. Am I?

Uhhhhhh. Out, out, blue haze. The haze. It must really smell in here. Can they smell the haze through blue walls? Probably. Wouldn't surprise me. A snooping sonic smelling device. Remember smoke dreams while a Chesterfield burns? Perry Como was it? These two have no idea who he was. So young.

I look at Sherry. Sherry now looks like Angie Dickinson in that old television police program. What was that program? What if she's really an undercover cop? Get out, Angie. Find another role. Come back Ann Margret. What if this is all a setup? What if Greg's an undercover cop? It happens. Everything happens. This happens. Under the covers happens. Shit happens. I shake my head. Something's loose in it. A screw?

I'm flat on my back on the floor, eyes closed. I push my fingers into the carpet. Deep pile. I've forgotten what color it is. So many samples we tried. I gave up. Whatever Janet wanted became okay with me. The carpet of many colors. I try to remember by its feel. Brown? Tan? Beige? What do I care? I float on the magic carpet as it changes colors, swirl through the air, a transcendental meditator, chanting mantras. Om. Om. Um. Yum.

"Want some pie?" I think it's Sherry. Do I want to stop floating for pie? For strawberry pie? For Sherry I'd do anything. Why? Because. Because. Because. It's the wonderful world of Oz. Greg's the wizard of pot. I look for the yellow brick road.

I land. I open my eyes and the light blasts through my skull. I sit up, air sick. I smile at Sherry's smile. It takes all my effort to be a mature English professor entertaining student guests in his home. The thought makes me laugh. A Stevie Wonder memory tape rolls, "My *chérie, amor...*"

"Oh, no," I groan, feeling the laughter coming again. I don't want to laugh. Nothing's funny.

Sherry picks up on it. Then Greg. Giggles become wet-eyed laughter.

"Stop!" I can't take it anymore. I hurt. Laughter finally fades, slows, dies, dead. I'm dead.

"Pie? Any one for pie?"

"High in the sky with my pie is my idea of..." I don't finish my song parody.

I can't help it, and I have no idea why, but I start laughing again. So do they. Who are these people in my home? I hardly know them and here I am experimenting, stepping out of myself. Or, into myself. Shouldn't I be ashamed, humiliated? They're still out there, building their case. Too late now.

"Mm, this is great." Greg extols on the pie he's eating. I watch him take another bite and show a face of pleasure. Sherry is also yumming. She's yummy. Can't seem to control my thoughts. Sorry, Janet. I don't want these unfamiliar cravings. Yes I do. I'm old but I still see. Please no.

Where have I been all my life? I see a large piece of strawberry pie on a dish in front of me, fork at the ready. I take a bite. It's the best bite of pie I have ever eaten in my whole entire life.

I tell them.

"The best bite of pie I have ever eaten in my entire life." I am sincere. Strawberries never tasted like this. Just now invented. Oh, crispy crust. Taste lives. Long live this taste!

Greg and Sherry say nothing, but nod and munch in agreement. We are all three having an orgiastic moment, no words needed, all in the same place, sharing, communicating at a level I never knew existed, intimate friends. I love this moment of sharing. I wonder why it has taken me so long to get here. My, god, I could have known this in my twenties. What a slow learner!

As an English major—professor—I should know about drugs and things first hand so I know what Kesey and Ginsberg are talking about, right? I mean, I'm branching out, right, into biology, right? Bio means life, right? And ology means the study of, right? So, I mean, this is a lab experiment to help me understand about a plant, the effects of a plant. The study of the life of a plant. Cannabis. Cause and effect, right? You two are my assistants. No, I'm the assistant getting first-hand information here, right? I'm learning about sativa and indica and kush and CBD and my ABCs. We couldn't do this in the school lab, could we? The government says no-no. No can do. Bad stuff. Ho-ho-ho. The fools on them. I mean the joke. Well, really the joke's on me. 'Cause I wasn't ready back when everyone was—well, anyway, I just didn't think it was right. Old school me. I still don't know about it being right, that's what this is all about, but…I stop, remembering the pie and eat some more.

"God, this is good."

"Way—to—go—Man." Greg stretches out the words, points his fork at me, laughs.

Sherry nods, smiles. She has pie on her face.

I reach over and wipe her chin, lick that finger clean. Yummy. Daring. Sherry looks at me. The look scares me a little. What did I just do?

"You should get stoned sometime with your wife and have sex," Greg tells me, scraping his plate with his fork trying not to leave any red traces.

I wish he hadn't said that. I don't know what to say. My sex life does not seem an appropriate subject for my students. Today we're studying plants.

"Yeah?" I hear myself say. Did I want that to be a question?

"Yeah. This stuff really heightens your sex buds, huh, Sherry." He doesn't really ask Sherry. Just says it. But she nods.

"Um, for sure. Very tactile—great orgasms."

Sherry said that? I don't know the girl and she's telling me about her orgasms? I look at her. She has a look on her face I can't decipher, not Ann-Margret, not Angie. I wonder what look is on my face. Can she decipher me? I shiver.

There's a silence I can hear, then Greg says, "Time for some music. This experiment of the senses can't be complete without music." He crawls over to the stereo system. "Brought the perfect CD." He pulls it from his jacket pocket—like magic—and inserts it in my CD player.

I recognize it. Ravel's "Bolero."

We sit in silence, supposedly listening. Maybe Greg and Sherry are. I'm not sure what I'm doing. I hear the music, but I don't, you know? I'm shivering but dripping wet down my armpits.

Greg has his arm around Sherry. She leans her head on his shoulder. Greg sees me looking, smiles. Come join us, I think he says. Or is it what I want to hear? I want my wife to be here.

A lie.

Sherry pats the floor, inviting me to sit by her. What are the boundaries here? Visions come. Time's gone. I'm gone. Does that mean there are no boundaries to this experiment? Did I set up a hypothesis? I'm not sure who I am. I see a fish taking bait, running with it, running, running, like my heart. I'm the fish. They are experimenting with me. I'm under the microscope. I'm their guinea pig. What's their hypothesis? Will I prove their theory? What do they want the headlines to be?

I sit next to her. Ravel continues rising, wide, circling. The Experiment—the big E is building, uniting us. I close my eyes, waiting, shivering. A hand rests on my leg. I know it's hers. I don't move. I want to stroke her butterfly. Afraid. Very afraid. What would Janet think? What does Greg think? Sherry's head leans on my shoulder now. Or is my head on her shoulder? My head tilts into soft smells of lavender—not the usual lab smell—the fragrance grows, permeating, blending into the closing, tightening circles of Ravel's repeating chords, drums taking over, taking me, my five senses now all one, no distinction between where I'm going and what is supposed to be as I lie back and Sherry's lips touch mine—me—and that's all I want, all that matters, not sure that's what is happening, not sure what I'm wanting to be happening is happening, not sure I haven't fallen back into time, not sure what Greg must think, not sure of anything. Does anything matter?

Forget Greg. He's just your teacher. Be the man. Feel only lavender. Feel all those lavender dances you think you missed…dig into the senses…

Something's wrong. The Bolero sounds strange. It's the ringing. It doesn't belong. There is no ringing in this piece, but it's there. Ravel's ringing. Distracting. Dissolving the lavender.

"Don't answer it," Greg says.

He's the teacher, but I must answer, because I know deep inside—it's my wife.

Janet's out there. She wants in. Do I want her in? Can she see what's happening? Have I done her wrong?

I crawl from the floor, where most of me wants to be, find the telephone from habit.

My voice sounds funny, Janet says. She wants to know why it took so long to answer. She was about to hang up. What are you doing? Are you okay? Is that Bolero playing? Is someone there?

I try to answer correctly, straight arrow. The Man. Big mistake. "Yes, it's Ravel and yes someone is here."

"Who?"

"Students."

"What students? What are they doing there so late? Why are you playing music?"

"They brought it to study by. We're experimenting."

"Experimenting? At home? What's going on? You sound so strange."

I sputter a laugh. "Nothing," I say. I laugh again, nervous, knowing nothing is the wrong answer. I look at Greg and Sherry. We start laughing, witless, uncontrolled laughter that I know brings fear to my wife, brings me tears, cold tears, washing away the experiment, washing away the lavender, washing away my experimental senses, opening my eyes, seeing through the blue haze the drying stains of strawberry pie on Janet's good white dishes.

Stretched out on the warm sand, Kevin leaned on one elbow watching his daughter play tag with the ocean. He smiled at her squeals of delight as she jumped back when the cool, foamy waves rushed toward her toes. When the water receded, her short, bare chubby legs took her forward to the ocean's edge, only to retreat again in fast backward steps as the waves dashed toward her. Sometimes she would bend down and splash the shallow water back upon itself, jump up and down, then repeat her game of tag.

She wore only the blue bottoms of a child's two-piece bathing suit, having refused to wear the small top that hid nothing at her age, wanting to be bare on top, "like daddy." He had laughed at her insistence, wondering how long before modesty would not allow her to stay bare in front of him. Holding her still, he rubbed the white sun cream over her face, back, chest, arms, legs, then let her loose to run to the water.

"Be careful, Cindy," he had yelled, realizing at once how needless and silly it sounded. He was right there. She never went deep enough for a wave to knock her down. Still, somewhere in the dark recesses of his mind lay all the fears that a father holds for a daughter and gives reason to say, "Be careful; please be careful."

Kevin saw Cindy look back at him, making sure he was still there. She gave a quick wave. He waved back, her assurance. She returned to her game.

Kevin liked coming to the beach after Labor Day. The hordes, all back at school or work, left long stretches of clean, tan sand nearly void of footprints. The weather was still warm and the azure sky cloudless. The aroma of suntan lotions still lingered in the air. How could that be? Ah, the two young women walking past him.

Both tall—women seemed taller these days—the skimpy suits they wore probably had less combined material than Cindy's bottoms. Early twenties he guessed, both parading their enviable, smooth bodies with even, photo-perfect tans for who ever cared to look. He cared to look. Female bodies like theirs he considered nature's works of art that allowed, even if just for that moment, an honest recognition of the primitive, universal feeling of pleasant sexual attraction, craving and need. Do women look at men with those same reactions?

Perfect bodies now, he thought, but what of later years when their smooth, hairless skin begins to wrinkle and fold and become brown blotched with possible melanomas?

But for now they commanded attention, and he gave it to them. They passed—

"What happened?"

"Whadaya think? I told him what I thought of him."

"No kidding. What'd he say?"

"He was all like…"

—and left him in their wake.

Wait. Come back. Kevin wanted to know what the one barely in blue said to him, whoever the "him" was. He followed her with his eyes, losing interest in her friend. She possessed that something beyond form that causes a man, no matter what age, to feel an instinctive yearning, like the line from an old song—"…it takes a long, tall, brown-skinned gal to make a preacher lay his Bible down." Something about her stride, her focused walk, her blonde hair cut short, almost like a man's, though she would never be taken for one. He wanted her to turn around so he could see her face again, to compare it to…

Pepper still crept into his thoughts from time to time; seeing someone in a checkout line, or maybe sitting across from him in a coffee shop, or with a friend of a friend, but mostly in the summer when he breathed in the combined scent of the sea and sun lotions, watched the girls in their summer undress, when he felt the sand, like her, fall through his fingers.

He met her at an impromptu beach party when he was about the age of the women passing by. In truth, he never really met her, that's what's so puzzling. She happened to be among the ten or twelve surfers at Rincon that day. He was sitting on his board waiting for the next strong swell. When he glanced at the surfer beside him, he was surprised. Not many women surfed in those days. Her wet, short, blond hair gave shape to her captivating face. She returned his staring with a blue-eyed smile that hit him like an unexpected ten-foot wave. When he saw her stand up on her board to take the ride in, her blue, one-piece swimsuit clinging to her body like flesh, he felt he'd witnessed an image of perfection and something in his being—what, he didn't understand and never experienced before— seduced him forever.

He missed some good rides watching her. Waiting for a wave in, he would paddle his board close to hers when he could. She smiled at him once again, but not with any recognition. He wanted to say something to her—ask her name—praise her surfing—express his feelings—anything that would connect them—but he didn't know what to say, or how to say it if he did. He drifted into a funk, sensed in himself imperfection, inferiority, an unwanted shyness.

Still…

The surf was beyond perfect and no one wanted the day to end. Toward evening, and without planning, they collectively found themselves piling driftwood for a fire. He and others shallow dived. He caught his first abalone after someone loaned him a long screwdriver and showed him how to quickly shove it under the shell before the hovering abalone suctioned itself to a rock. He hoped she had seen him bring it up. Look at what I caught! See me!

Someone managed to catch a couple of lobsters. Beer appeared from nowhere. One guitar player, then another, brought everyone around the fire that grew bigger and brighter as the sun dropped away. He kept looking for her—at her. When he asked around, someone told him her name: Pepper. Was that her real name? Yes. No. No one seemed sure.

Pepper.

Yes. Oh, yes.

Riveted, he watched her sing and sway her head and shoulders with the music. He watched her laugh. He watched her playfully kick sand at someone who teased her. Kick sand at me! The firelight reflected in her eyes bewitched him. Bewitched, yes, a silly-good word. He watched the tip of her tongue in the corner of her mouth as she helped pound and cook the abalone. She put a piece of abalone in the mouth of a surfer everyone called Killer Kahuna, conqueror of waves and women. My abalone! Mine! He watched her shiver and accept a sweatshirt from him. He watched the two of them leave the fire and fade into the dark. He watched for their return.

He watched in vain, never to see her again.

But she left on him an invisible tattoo that continues to bear an obsession of her that always brings a flash of despondency. No, despair might not be the right word. Why? Even now he still can't find a word for it. For some feelings there are no words. He only knows she had inexplicably touched him forever, and that something, whatever it was, continues to dwell inside him and rises up whenever he sees an iteration of her. How many times had he tried to understand his reaction?

Over the years he'd tried to convince himself his reaction was obvious. He would never be a Kahuna, in or out of the water, never the one to walk away with a Pepper. She symbolized something unattainable, a representation of a life he would never experience simply because of who he was and never could be. Pepper, someone he never talked to, never knew he existed, somehow awoke in him the loss of his unconscious innocence with an awareness of what he was not.

And what of Pepper? What happened to her? Did she enjoy whatever happened that night? Was disappearing into the dark with Kahuna memorable for her, or would she even remember that night now? Was she taken advantage of? Or was she taking advantage of her position? Could she have been aware of her power over him? And if she ever learned how he, Kevin, felt, how she touched him, how she set a pattern in his life, would she understand or care?

Oh, he'd known many women since then, and Cindy's mother was a brag-of-a catch herself. No complaints there. One could say he'd done quite well. And he could say with honesty that he felt happy in his marriage.

And yet...

Pepper.

He'd been looking at Cindy, but not seeing her. He didn't know how long she'd been waving at him. He waved back, smiled.

Cindy, tired of her game, began running toward him, her quick pace suddenly slowing—slowing—slowing. Kevin sat up and watched, amazed, as her short, chubby child legs began a gradual transformation into long, smooth, womanly ones, stemming down from narrow hips almost covered by her low slung, blue-bottomed suit, exposing her navel sunk into a taut waist that hour-glassed up toward firm breasts now held in place by the top she had discarded to be like daddy, flicking her wet, short blond hair away from her alluring face, a wide, white smile set off by her perfect end-of-summer tan bringing him a strong scent of sea and summer lotions.

"Oh, be careful," he heard himself say.

FRENCH DIP

Barnaby Triller strolled the narrow, time-smoothed cobblestone lanes of old Arles bringing to life those quiet pictures of old French cities he'd studied so often in his art books. He stopped to touch and photograph an antiquated stone arch that held up the two old buildings he walked between. A Roman leftover, no doubt, probably forgotten and unappreciated. It was a cliché, he knew, but here he felt he'd stepped back in time, a genteel period he felt more suited to, a time when great art was at its peak. Passing by weathered wooden doors, he felt a touch of envy, wanted to see behind them. If only he could enter one of these passageways into a hundred years ago. Perhaps bump into Van Gogh or...

Barnaby snapped back to the present as he rounded a narrow bend. Energetic accordion music rose from somewhere in the crowds seated under clumps of large red, yellow, and blue-white sun umbrellas. Colored paper lamps dangled from overhead wires strung between large plane trees on either side of the square.

Was it a festival of some sort? He checked his tourist office information map and discovered he'd wandered into *la place du Forum*. Apparently, several restaurants had set up to serve outdoor lunch. Yes, so very French.

He thought to turn back up the quiet lane. Crowds were so bothersome. But tired from walking all morning, and with the mixture of food aromas awakening his hunger, he decided to find a table, off to the side if possible. Afterward he'd search for the two ancient Corinthian columns supposedly still intact that his map indicated stood near the square. They might be worth photographing to show his students.

It took him a moment to realize three different cafés, crammed together under the plaza's thickly, green-leafed plane trees, each distinguished by the different colored umbrellas and matching chairs, vied for business. Chalk-written menus, placed on wobbly shoulder-high stands near each color break, announced that particular restaurant's menu du jour.

He picked a section featuring chicken and sat at an empty table under a yellow umbrella. When the waiter came for his order, he learned that he was sitting where the menu was rabbit, not chicken. Though not fond of rabbit, but too embarrassed to move, he ordered a *demi-pichet* of red wine to go with it.

After the waiter left, Barnaby figured out his mistake. The chicken menu section was one table away under a blue-white umbrella. It would have been so easy to move over just one table, there, where that woman sat alone.

He looked more closely at her. An attractive fortyish. His age. A few slight crow wrinkles around the eyes, olive complexion, a couple of faint lines on each side of her mouth that might break into dimples if she smiled. She looked his way. Barnaby flushed and examined his fingernails.

It did feel good to sit for a bit, he decided, leaning back in his seat. Having spent the morning photographing the old Roman amphitheater, the Museum of Pagan Art, and the *Alyscamps*, he had found Arles a bit disappointing, especially since Van Gogh lived and painted here for part of his life. One expected more references and tributes to the man than window posters of his sunflowers. All he'd found so far was that ugly greenish monument in the park that looked like a death mask stuck on a rock slab. But this was, after all, the town that petitioned to have the poor lonely soul committed. He had taken a few shots of the mask at different angles, hoping he'd find more than that to use in his art classes.

So here he was, following the tourist map, even though being a tourist was the last thing he wanted to believe of himself. After the Italian fiasco two years ago with that boring tour group of art teachers, he swore his next trip would be sans anyone. No more being herded around with people he didn't know, with time deadlines, sharing hotel rooms, having to eat whatever was on the menu for the group, nothing but teacher talk, no chance to meet other people. This time he wanted to select his own hotels, stay in one place if he wished, eat and drink when and wherever he wanted. He'd even taken a night refresher course in French before he left. He was here to learn, to find and develop materials for his art courses.

Barnaby found that staring at the woman was quite unavoidable since their tables faced each other. She had a rather classic profile at a certain angle. He began examining her as he would a painting or a sculpture. He studied her short, almost curly, light-brown hair brushed back, showing well-shaped ears with small, dangling silver earrings, but he couldn't make out their design. Her sunglasses, pushed up over her forehead into her hair, exposed a tanned, oval face. No makeup, well, maybe a touch of something light on her lips. Nice, subtle. Her almost sleeveless white blouse, a low square cut at the neck, framed a necklace with pendant that lay just in that shallow where her breasts began to mound.

The more he studied her the more Barnaby found himself intrigued, attracted by what he perceived as a very sad, perhaps despondent woman. He did have training in observing detail, after all. Something about her touched him. What exactly? A love affair recently ended? A death in the family? Perhaps a nasty divorce. Something must have hurt her deeply, he felt certain.

The woman leaned over the side of her chair and reached into her bag on the ground. Barnaby thought she might be reaching for a handkerchief (was she about to cry?), but instead she pulled a caramel tipped cigarette from a pack and lit it expertly with a small gold lighter.

He lost a little respect for her, not at all liking the way she blew the smoke from the corner of her mouth. She placed one arm across her waist and rested the elbow of her other arm on it, straight up, wrist bent, long fingers holding the cigarette out like a flag. A practiced pose? Did she think she looked sophisticated?

He watched her nervously twist the lighter around in her other hand, staring at it for a moment, then slip it back in her purse. Barnaby ventured the lighter had been a gift from a lover who had jilted her, a sad momento she couldn't bear to discard. Yes, she was sad and lonely. He understood.

He forgave her for the cigarette.

His appraisal established her as a professional of some sort. Certainly attractive, yes, certainly that. Was she French or a lone foreign traveler like himself? He decided she was French.

"Excuse me, but I'm an art professor making my way around the sites of Arles. I notice you're alone. Would you like to join me for a look at *Les Alyscamps*? Both Van Gogh and Gauguin painted the old Roman cemetery, you know. Quite differently, too…"

He squirmed deeper into his chair. How preposterous. Silly. Ridiculous. Not like him at all. He forced his eyes from the woman.

When her waiter brought her a *demi pichet*, he couldn't help watching as she poured the white wine into a glass, sat back, leaned one elbow on the arm of her chair, wrist bent, cigarette held out, that pose again. Her other hand reached for her glass, brought it to her mouth. Absently, she rolled the edge of the wineglass lightly back and forth across her bottom lip, then sipped.

Barnaby shifted uncomfortably in his chair.

She set her glass down, glancing his way. His eyes dropped, his face flamed. He squirmed about in his chair, caught.

But wait. Caught at what, exactly? So he was looking at her. So what? Why should he feel guilty? The French always stared openly. Anyway, looking at people in these crowded squares is unavoidable, one café running into the other as they do. He sat up in his seat, annoyed. Why did he always find it easier to be an unobserved observer?

Barnaby poured himself wine from the pitcher he didn't remember his waiter bringing. He hoped she wasn't still looking his way. He feared looking hers.

Fear? Yes. But fear of what?

He wriggled in a surge of anger at his meekness. He crossed his legs once, twice.

The meek will never inherit the earth the way you're acting. Why don't you look at her, nod, smile? What are you afraid she'll do?

As sly as he could, he looked her way again. He couldn't be mistaken about her sad demeanor. He sensed in her a something he sensed in himself.

Maybe she'd like company. His French was passable.

She was concealing her vulnerability, each elbow bent and resting on the chair arms, with her glass of wine in one hand and her cigarette in the other. Lovely nails, manicured to a slight point, clear polish. With both arms set back as they were, he could see her nipples faintly outlined, a fullness from behind pushing against her thin blouse. If only he could see the rest of her hidden under the table. Her tanned legs were probably crossed, one slightly swinging, knees and lower thigh exposed just at the edge of her skirt.

He averted his eyes rather than be discovered again and sipped at his wine without tasting it. There, on a pedestal at the other end of the plaza stood a statue of Frederic Mistral, a hero of Provence. Pretending interest, he held her face in his mind. He liked her nose, Grecian, a neck worthy of fine sculpting marble. She could have posed for the classicists.

His eyes fixed on Mistral's hat, Barnaby pictured her in her twenties. Then, of course, her hair was blonder from the sun and her eyes had a clear, blue-green sparkle. A dimpled smile. Straight, even, white teeth. A tan with just a bikini strip of white around her hips. Her breasts fit perfectly into the palms of his hands. One hand slid down her glistening body, her skin copper smooth, her belly slightly sunk in as she lay prone on her back, one knee bent up. His pleasure rose as he traced his middle finger around her small, sunken navel, then moved down one thigh, back up to her navel, down the other thigh, back up to her navel…

"*Voila, monsieur!*"

His lunch slid in front of him.

He stared at half a roasted rabbit and something he didn't recognize. He was still studying it when his waiter returned with a small silver tray full of fries. Another quick "*Voila, monsieur, bon appétit,*" and the waiter disappeared.

With a loud sigh he hoped she didn't hear, Barnaby cut into his rabbit and took a bite, keeping the fork in his left hand, knife in the right, like the Europeans. With clandestine peeks her way between bites, he wondered if she thought he was French. She is, he decided, watching her eat her salad by rolling the lettuce neatly on her fork with her knife. Her mouth opened, accepted the bite with eyes down, lips closed around it. She slipped the naked fork from between her pursed lips, slowly.

Barnaby shivered.

She looked straight at him just as a piece of rabbit slipped off his fork and fell to his plate before it got to his opened mouth. Keeping his chagrined and flushed face down, he took aim and stabbed his fork through the fallen bite, wanting the rabbit to feel death again. His face lowered into his plate, chewing without taste, aware now of the dampness under his arms.

But he had to look up again.

Oh, god! She was still staring at him! She was laughing at him. Or, was that a smile? A smile for him? Really? Could she possibly be…?

A strange, new courage braced his body.

Be bold. For once. Find out.

Barnaby put down his knife and fork. He pushed his chair back and stood up, knees weak. Yes, she was smiling at him. He began practicing the French he would use.

Wait.

No. No, she wasn't. She was looking beyond him. He watched as she smiled perfect white teeth, yes, slight dimples, stood up, stretched out her smooth, bronzed arms to greet a well-dressed man who approached from behind Barnaby. They kissed on both cheeks and then the mouth. They sat down, the man's back now totally obstructing Barnaby's view of the woman.

Barnaby, brushing nothing off his seat with his napkin, sat down and stared at his half empty plate. No longer hungry and not caring that the menu price entitled him to cheese and dessert, he called the waiter and settled his bill.

He didn't look back, but he did hear the woman and man laugh just as he noticed the ancient Corinthian columns mentioned on the tourist map.

Yes, just there, beyond Mistral's statue.

SPUMINGS

T. C. Dash awoke knowing that something imperative—what exactly he couldn't say—would occur by mail today changing his life forever.

Too early—Dash nevertheless slipped on his worn slippers and frayed plaid robe with a hole in the left pocket—and labored—his arthritis you know—down the slanted cracked concrete driveway—to his battered mailbox set atop a thin leaning metal pole, missing letters on one side—

"T space C space space A space H"

Today—Dash decided—with more conviction about anything since his wife's sudden passing—he must make certain the mailbox reads—

"T space C space DASH"

Yes—there must be no mistake—not today—please not today.

Dash had trouble opening the rusty flap door on the mailbox—uncooperative bone muscle joints. After tug—tug—tug—pull—it opened. His bony brown-spotted hand crawled like a spider to the end of the metal box—nothing. He bent with a body creak—looked in—proving with certainty its emptiness.

Hoping he wasn't already too late—Dash looked down the street. No mail truck—only a neighbor's car parked across the street. He fumbled his blue-veined hands into his robe pockets—the one with a hole in it so he played with the hole making it bigger—then labored up the driveway—wheezing—unaware he was making the noise—loud wheezes—by the time he reached the top.

In the house—wheeze—wheeze—he stared—(pick an appropriate adverb here)— out the window—wanting more than life—yes—that's right—more than life—for the mail truck to arrive. But the untrimmed blood-red bougainvillea obfuscated his view—so he turned up his hearing aids—yes, both ears—to better listen for the truck.

Thinking he heard it—Dash dashed—well—as best his hunched bent body could—remember his arthritis—back down the slanted cracked concrete and pull—pull-tug—opened the little flap door. Nothing—again—only blood on his finger from his pull-tug on the little door flap—no awareness nor concern with how it happened. Whatever he had heard had disappeared.

Another laborious wheeze—same wheeze sounds—back to the house while dripping—Dash paid no attention— small blood drops.

Back in the house a remembrance of thoughts past—Oh—right—fix the mailbox!

Finding a red felt-tipped marker—he noticed it matched the blood on his fingers— from the old days grading innumerable unmemorable student essays—well—not all—a few were quite good if he wanted to be honest—Dash labored through another painful trip to the mailbox. The red ink was difficult to read against the faded black—but one side of the box now read—and he felt much relieved—

"T space C space dAsH."

He realized his d should be a capital—a small capital D—his **s** too small—but oh well—any fool can tell what the word is—Dash—so he raised the red metal flag on the side of his mailbox to signal a pick up—so the mail carrier would know to stop. That's what he wanted—he wanted it to stop. So simple—but he was wrong about the simple.

He shuffle-wheezed back to the house and stood—even though worn out now—in the opened doorway—waiting—and listening—for the white mail truck with a red and a blue stripe along the sides. Wasn't there an eagle's head on it? Yes—he was sure an eagle's head was painted somewhere on the truck—the side would be most logical—silly to paint one on the top.

As Dash grew more anxious—the more his certainty grew that this was the day—he felt it body and soul—mostly body, yes—still, not to deny the soul—so he took a kitchen chair—chrome plated with a gray patterned leatherette seat and back—and dragged it—unaware of the irritating scraping noise along the broken concrete—louder than those proverbial fingers on the chalkboard—same feeling—down the slanted driveway—placed it next to the mailbox—somehow the door had flopped open again—and sat.

After a few noddings off to wherever people waiting for the mail go—it began to drizzle. Still—Dash sat—not wanting to miss something he knew—desired—craved now—had to do with the mail. The rain fell on him gentle-like—just light—clear—tiny beads covering his thinning gray hair—eyelashes—nose—robe—toes of his slippers. Miniature beads grew in number—and left Dash feeling—well—wet.

Across the street—a neighbor lady saw him sitting there—thinking him foolish—yet understanding about his wife's sudden death—and his strange behavior since—and yelled to him—"You're getting soaked!"

"No matter,"—he hoarsed back—"Something imperative—is going to happen when the mail comes—I mustn't miss it."

A nice neighbor—he couldn't remember her name—his passed wife always had to remind him—now she couldn't—brought him an umbrella.

"I'm not going out—so use my umbrella." Foolish man—he's never recovered from his wife's death. He's going to catch his death.

"Thank you—you're a nice neighbor." He stood up—gave a slight bow—and took the umbrella. "I would get mine—but it's crucial I don't miss the mail today."

He sat on his soaked kitchen chair—holding his neighbor's open umbrella over him—shivered—his attention focused down the street.

His nice neighbor shook her head—sighed in a manner that meant poor man—and returned home.

Soon—a relative term—the rain became—a downpour. Water—from a drain spout—ran—gushed is a better word—down his slanted cracked concrete driveway and into the street where he sat—as you know by now—waiting for the mail. It wasn't long—another relative term—before the street gutter filled with running water—which now spilled over the curb and the tops of his soaked slippers.

Dash heard tires—splashing through the wet streets—peeked out from under the umbrella. At last—he thought—at last—the mail. Imagine his joy.

But—he was wrong—just a car that splashed water on him—his chair—and his neighbor's umbrella.

Dash began to shiver more. Still—he did not want to miss what must be coming for him—the heartfelt—and soul-felt—belief that something—something no one could put into words—not me, not you—something only he could experience— had some connection with the mail.

Imagine rain falling fast— so fast that Dash can barely see. Again he hears the sound of tires fighting the street water. Then— there it is—even in the rain with failing vision—the unmistakable white mail truck with a red and a blue stripe! And—yes—an eagle's head—white/blue—though not a good likeness.

The nice neighbor lady looked out her window and—even through all that heavy rain—noticed the beaming joy on old Dash's face just before the mail truck stopped. Briefly—again a relative time term—say less than ten seconds—he was hidden from her view by the truck with the faux white on blue eagle's head.

When the mail truck pulled away—Dash's mailbox door hung open—red flag now swung down loose— barely attached—the d now washed away in the rain—the kitchen chair now vacant.

The nice neighbor lady— she supposed she should be happy for Dash now—accepted that whatever just happened was his business alone—but did wonder if she'd ever get her umbrella back.

"Call me and it's all over," Nguyen says expressionless. His hand with the three gold rings spreads flat next to his cards on the green felt tabletop.

Is he bluffing? I can't see his eyes through those dark wrap-around glasses. I like to see a person's eyes when I'm playing poker, especially when the pot's over two million dollars.

Yeah, I've come this close, the last round after four days here in Vegas at "Glitter Gulch's" Binion's Horseshoe, home to the World Championship of Poker. And yeah, I'm nervous. Who'd have thought I'd be in the league with guys like Patrik Antonius, Phil Ivory, Antonio Esfandiari, or Sam Trickett. They're real pros, man. But here I am, Sammy Damona, one step away from the biggest pot I've ever seen.

And I need it. Alimony. Child support. IRS screaming down my neck. It was all I could do to scrape up enough to get in the game. I shouldn't even be here. I mean, they aren't going to give me my teaching job back, not after I skipped out to play in this poker championship.

But I'll worry about that later. Right now I don't know what to do. I hold three 10s, two showing, one under. Nguyen shows three 8s. Does he have the other 8 under? Does he want me to call him because he knows it's over?

He just sits there, poker-faced behind those black glasses, waiting. He's cool and rich and I resent him. I want to beat him, and not just for the money. The money's nice, but that's not why I play the game. I want to be a winner for once in my life.

The sweat rolls down from my armpits. My shirt sticks to my back. I think, "Oh, Great God of All Cards in the Home of the Royal Flush, tell me what to do here. Do I call him?" Like a little kid, I pray, "Let me win this game and I promise I'll…"

A cigar-smoking spectator blows blue-gray smoke out over the table where it swirls, hovers in front of my face, then turns white and just hangs there like a solid hunk.

At first, I think the pressure has me seeing things. Easy like, I reach out toward the smoke and touch it. Holy King of Cards! It's hard—solid cold—and I don't want to believe it.

I look around the table. Not only has the smoke frozen, but so has everybody in the room. I mean, they are icicle stiff, like time stopped and they got caught in their last act of movement. The room gets colder.

I can't believe what's happening. I'm stunned!

"How badly do you want to win, Sammy?"

I look around. My jaw drops. The cigar smoker, wearing a cowboy hat, a red flannel shirt and weathered Levis, comes unfrozen, smiles, takes another big puff, and blows a smoke ring around the frozen cloud. It just hangs there.

I blink about ten times.

"I asked you a question, Sammy. How badly do you want to win?"

"I…ah…I…ah…"

"Sammy, Sammy, Sammy. Come on, now. You called for help. I'm here to help. But I need to know how badly you want to win before I can help."

Dry mouthed, and still distracted by the hanging frozen smoke, I accomplish a weak, "Whadayamean?"

"Not real quick, are you? Great, glittering, grandiose casinos, how did you manage to get this far in the tournament?" He sighs. "Look. You want to win. I can help. I could have Nguyen drop dead of a heart attack. I could keep everybody frozen while you go take a look at your opponent's cards. I could change the cards in your hand to beat his. Know what I'm saying?"

I feel my dropped jaw move. "You could do all that?"

"Sammy, Sammy, look at me. I'm King of the Aces. Now, the question is, if I help you, what do you do for me?"

King of the Aces? I look again at the stiff crowd and frozen smoke. "You? You need help?"

"Yes. Afraid so. I've got all the new Native American casinos popping up, and then Vegas reproducing the whole damn world here on the strip, then there's the new river boats, yeah, gaming's on the rise. I could use some help answering calls like yours." He flicks the cigar ashes, which turn into ice crystals and tinkle when they hit the ashtray.

"Yeah, well, how? I mean, what could I possibly do to help you?" I can't believe I'm having this conversation. Should someone call 911? I don't let him see me pinch my hand to make sure I haven't spaced out under the pressure.

"Here's the thing, Sammy. I can't keep up with all the calls for help. Like yours." He smiles. "Now, if you were to be my protégé, agree to assist when I get calls like yours…"

"Assist you? Whoa, man, I don't have your power."

"I can delegate."

My head gets what he's saying, spins at the possibility!

"Yeah, sure. You must be on call whenever I need you, which, granted, is most all the time. And I pick who you work with and who wins. I always call the shots. Deal?"

Me, with such power! And two million bucks! My god, how that would change my luck! My life! Yeah, I'd be a proud winner, a somebody.

Then comes the dawn. "But what good is winning the pot if I have to work for you full time?"

"Comin' around, aren't you? Okay. Point taken. Look, I'll give you a year to spend your winnings. You can have anything you want—women, cars, jewelry, clothes, travel, you name it. End of the year, you come to work for me."

I feel the temptation. I want to win more than anything. I mean, that's over two million bucks on the table! That's the biggest pot I've ever been in. It took everything I had and more to scrape a stake together. I could kiss off my financial debt forever! Never have to teach again. My ex would get off my back. I could see my kid. And my god, I'd be famous in the poker world! One of the big boys. My name spoken at all the big games. Yeah, a poker champ for all history, name on the plaque. My dream come true.

Then he sweetens the pot.

"Okay, look. I'll even throw in a month off every year. Paid. Free to do or go where you want."

I'm ready to say yes.

"But," he says before I can speak, "no more playing poker—ever. Zilch. Nada. Rien." He puts the dead cigar in his mouth and pushes back his hat. "So that's the deal, Sammy. Make up your mind. This game's gotta end. I got other appointments."

What he says sinks in. I'd never be able to play poker again. Never compete. Plus he might assign me to help some jerk win, some player who doesn't even know the game. So I'm thinking, I'm only a card away from being a champ on my own without his help. One card away from a two-million-dollar pot. So I try a new tack. "Couldn't we work out something else?"

He shrugs. "Well, Sammy, for two million bucks, you know, it's gotta be good. Offer me."

I think for a minute, which is hard to do, as you can imagine. So, out comes, "How about I give a fourth of the pot to your favorite charity and I can keep playing poker?"

The King sputters. "Are you tapioca or what? Charity? Charity's what I'm offering you! If I let you play, how's that help my problem? Too many of you playing now!"

I try hard, but I can't think of anything to persuade him. So I have to tell him no, man, I can't do it. I love poker too much to do it his way.

He shrugs, gives me a look like I'm some kind of fool. "Remember, Sammy, you called for me. I didn't call you. Last chance. One… two…"

Then snap. The hazy blue smoke is back floating around the table, casino sounds fill the room again, and everybody's all normal like they were. Nguyen's still stoic, tapping his stacked cards with one ringed finger, eyes still hidden behind those dark glasses. If only he knew what I'd just experienced, that smug look of his would disappear.

I look through the swirling smoke at those shades of his, and I see what I have to do.

Pushing out all my chips, I call Nguyen.

He flips his cards.

Four 8s.

Nguyen takes off his glasses, real cool like. His mouth twitches in a superior smirk as he pulls in the pot. Two million bucks. And I'm tapped. Out. Finito.

Before they all crowd around him, I catch Nguyen turn, give a sly wink at the spectator with the hat and cigar—yeah, the King of the Aces—who nods at Nguyen, then looks at me, shrugs his shoulders, and disappears into the casino crowd leaving a trail of blue haze.

It all sinks in and I start this crazy laugh.

At what, I'm not exactly sure.

"Hello."

"Hi. Is Ted there?"

"Ted? Who's calling?"

"Is this Nancy?

"Yes. Who's this?"

"Oh, hi, Nancy. I don't know if you remember me, a voice out of the past. Noah Bly, from Woodriver. Ted and I…"

"I remember."

"Wasn't sure. It's been awhile, hasn't it?"

"Yes."

"Too long, I know. Well, here's the thing. I'm en route to San Francisco and had this stopover in Phoenix, so I thought I'd call while I'm here at the airport. Will Tee be home soon? I'd like to talk to him."

"Nancy?"

"Ted…Ted died, Noah."

"What?"

"Seven years ago."

"Oh, god, no. I had no idea. I'm so sorry. Seven years ago?"

"Yes."

"What happened? I mean, how?"

"Heart. He'd had two angioplasties before the final attack."

"Seven years ago. Why, he was only fifty then. I had no idea he had heart trouble."

"Well, it's not like you kept in touch, Noah."

"I know. I know. I mean—it's just so unexpected. I don't want to believe it."

"We had no idea where you were, how to let you know. I wasn't even sure you cared."

"Well, of course, I care. It's just that time—I don't know where it went. I kept meaning to call after I moved to St. Louis, really, but, you know…"

"Nancy?"

"Yes?"

"Oh, I thought we got disconnected."

"No."

"Listen, I'm really sorry if this call is, you know, bringing up sad memories for you. I wish I'd known."

"Why? What would you have done?"

"Ah, well, I don't know. Visit? Been there for him somehow? He always was for me. I think about him—and you—so often. I mean, Ted and I were best friends in school. I named my son after Ted. Did you know that? Ted Stanley Bly."

"No, I didn't. We didn't know you had a son."

"I must have written."

"No. If you did, Ted never mentioned it. And I'm sure he would have."

"Well, that would have been—lord, no. Has it really been that long since we've been in touch?"

"Longer. Ted often wondered about you, where you were, what you were doing. He thought you were friends."

"Well, of course. We are—were. The best. I told Ted, my son, all about Ted, your Ted. I mean, my god, he probably saved my life twice. Did he ever tell you about that one winter, we were about sixteen, ice-skating on a golf course lake and I fell through? The skates and wet wool clothes pulled me down. I panicked, thought I'd bought it. But Ted, man, he kept his cool, took off his jacket, lay flat on the ice, threw me one of the sleeves, and pulled me through the cracked ice until it was shallow enough for me to crawl out with his help."

"He told me."

"And one summer, we were sailing a little Snipe when this wind comes up out of nowhere, fills the main so fast it snaps the boom and knocks me overboard. I don't even remember how he managed to handle the boat and help me get back on. I was hit pretty hard, maybe out cold for a few seconds. Even now I'm not sure how he did it. But Ted…

"Nancy? You still there?"

"What do you want me to say, Noah?"

"I—nothing, I guess. I get the feeling I'm upsetting you. Sorry, if I am. So, how are you? I mean, you sound—well—not well."

"I'm having some respiratory problems."

"Oh, sorry. Are you seeing a good doctor? Anything I can do?"

"Listen, Noah, it's a little late for you to be getting concerned, don't you think?"

"Well, I'm, you know, interested. I'm so behind—so stunned—sorry."

"Nancy? You there?"

"Yes?"

"Do you have any children?"

"Two boys, men now."

"Oh, that's good. That's good. Are they close by? Do you get to see them often? My son—I don't know where he is."

"Look, Noah, I don't really know you all that well. In fact, I hardly know you at all except for what Ted's told me. I only met you a month before our wedding, remember. I knew you as Ted's best man. Thought you were his best friend. Then you left town and we've never heard from you since."

"I don't know where the time went. Life just went on, you know? It wasn't like I didn't think about you guys. I did. Often. I never had a friend like Ted before—or since. I miss him."

"A good friend would have kept in touch with Ted. He said he wondered about you, even worried about you. Shouldn't you remember old friends, especially the ones who save your life?"

"But I do remember. That's why I'm calling."
"You're a little late, Noah."

"Nancy?"

"Nancy, don't hang up, please. Please, Nancy—I'm really sorry."

"Nancy?"

"Ted? Ted? Please? You there? I need…"

"Listen, Ted, I need to talk to you, buddy. Yeah, it's been a long time, I know, and Nancy's pissed and I'm sorry, but let's get caught up while I'm here, okay? They'll be calling my flight pretty soon. Listen, I miss you. I'm really sorry I never got in touch before. I honestly don't know why I didn't. I don't, ya' know? I kept thinking about calling. Really. I just never got around to it. Meant to. Anyway, things were bad and I didn't want to whine. You know how that goes. But I should have called. I know that. Anyway, here I am. As soon as I got off the plane I called before something happened to keep me from calling. I wish I could stay in Phoenix overnight, get together and go over old times, but I have to give a presentation at a conference tonight. A big shot in this organization you never heard of. And it's all your fault, buddy. You're the one who talked me into being an engineer, remember? Well, it's been okay. You were right. Professional side is going fine, but—well, my personal life—not so good. That's what I need to talk to you about. Look, I don't have any real friends but you. Oh, I've got colleagues, but, you know, they're not—friends—like us—like it was…you know? Wife divorced me. Yeah. So-called friends have taken Beth's side, it seems. And my son, Tee—don't know where he is. Doesn't want me to know. So, see, so many things I need to talk to you about. You always had good insight into things, a good listener—a real friend—and I—I need a friend, Tee, advice. Things aren't…

"But, hey, enough about me. Still at Motorola? Two kids—boys, Nancy tells me. That's great. Oh-oh, they're calling my flight. Listen, gotta run. Give Nancy my best. Let's keep in touch, get caught up. Yeah. Promise."

When Alfred Nipple walked into his classroom Thursday morning and saw everything he'd written in green on the whiteboard the night before had been erased, his reaction, even for him, was out of the ordinary. Ask the faculty their opinion of him and they'd agree with Hal, the history teacher. "Nipple's a milquetoast, a bore, a sad sack, a wimp." Coach Windsocky summed it up. "The last guy I'd pick for my team." Alice, the math teacher, said, "He's shy."

Most of the faculty tried to be friendly. After a few years, they gave up. Alfred Nipple would shuffle into the faculty lounge, the staff would acknowledge him, he'd nod, mumble "good morning," then sit by himself slipping cucumber sandwiches from a brown bag and sipping what looked like tomato juice from his Roy Rogers thermos.

The staff made fun of him. Not to his face. Not much, anyway. With a name like A. Nipple, it was hard not to tease him.

The students never voted him the most popular teacher on campus, though he was a frequent topic of conversation. They knew if they asked the right questions, got him going, they could kill a whole period.

Alfred Nipple knew his stuff, his presentations formidable. He couldn't teach without a whiteboard. Excited while explaining some chemical equation, Nipple would begin writing on the board, his back to his class, forgetting them, writing on and on until every inch of the board was covered green with formulas and diagrams. Out of space, he'd stop, flustered, and stare at the wall as if he wanted to write on it. Turning around, flabbergasted the class was there, he'd pace back and forth mumbling until the bell.

It astonished everyone when Alfred Nipple banged through the faculty lounge door Thursday morning, standing in his seersucker suit and crooked bow tie demanding to know who'd done it.

"Done what, Al?" several voices asked.

"Someone deliberately erased an hour's worth of work I placed on the board last night." His tweety voice wobbled.

"Gee, Nips, that's too bad," sniggered the coach.

"I demand to know who did it."

"Maybe a custodian?" Alice suggested tenderly.

"He'd never do that. I wrote 'SAVE' in big, green letters and drew a circle around it."

"A mischievous student?" Hal suggested.

"I wrote it last night after everyone left."

"Why do you suspect us, Al?"

The room got very quiet with that question. Al, seething, turned and left.

That was the last time the staff ever saw Alfred Nipple or heard his voice.

Early Friday morning before classes began, a distraught custodian asked Principal Bayard to come to Mr. Nipple's classroom.

"Very odd," the principal said after the custodian pointed it out.

"That's not all," the custodian replied. "Every damn whiteboard in the school, upstairs and down, is filled in the same way!"

When they got to their classrooms, each teacher discovered the word "save," meticulously printed in very small letters with a circle drawn around it, repeated over and over and over in various pastel colored chalk, covering every inch of space on every whiteboard.

Rumors started circulating. Hal, the history teacher, said after what Nipple did he's too embarrassed to come back and left for parts unknown, probably changing his name. Coach Windsocky, angry because the school went without chalk for several weeks, making football scrimmages impossible, hoped "the Nipper" had turned to chalk dust and been blown away in a big wind. Alice, ever sympathetic, believed Alfred Nipple vanished to the other side of the whiteboard where she's certain he's a happier man.

Wash—him—off. Wash—him—off.

Velma, too intent on scrubbing, didn't hear her low mumbles. She welcomed the sting of the fine spray from the showerhead, the coarseness of the brush turning her skin from pinkish to red.

Soap every inch, brush, rinse. More, more between the legs. Soap, brush, rinse.

Exhausted, skin tingling, she dropped the soap, stopped scrubbing and stood face up under the shower, wishing the water could wash it—him—away, down the drain, out of her life.

What have you done? No, you know what you've done. The real question is why? Curiosity? Envy? Horny? A need to feel attractive, younger? Seduced by youth? Boredom? Striking a blow for sexual freedom? All of the above?

The water turned colder. She decided she would stand in the shower until the water froze her to death.

And you, a psych teacher. You, of all people, should know better. How can you call yourself a professional? All those years of classes and training. Fat lot of good. Up for tenure next year. You'll never get it now. And how are you going to face your classes tomorrow? How can you look him in the eyes, sitting there, knowing? What if he's told other students in the class? Why did you do it? Do you realize you just shot down your career?

Velma shivered, not sure how long she'd been under the cold water, and turned off the faucets. When she stepped out of the shower she reached for a bath towel that wasn't there. She'd forgotten to get one from the closet, so had to walk across the bathroom, dripping water all over the cold, black-tiled floor.

After drying off, Velma opened the bathroom door and entered the bedroom. Only...

This isn't your bedroom.

Velma stood in the doorway looking at a queen-sized bed that wasn't hers, night tables on either side that weren't hers, a mahogany dresser that wasn't hers, and flowered curtains that weren't hers.

Where are you, Velma?

Arriving home, she had rushed to the bathroom to take a shower, had torn off her clothes, thrown them on the floor, wanting to burn them. They were gone now, along with her bedroom!

Perplexed and a bit dizzy, Velma stepped back into the bathroom. She realized now that the bathroom wasn't hers either. She opened the medicine cabinet, avoiding her face in the mirror. Unfamiliar jars and bottles. Nothing of hers. And no glass on the sink with her toothbrush.

My god! You're in the wrong apartment! But how? And where are your clothes? Your purse and briefcase?

"Is anyone here?"

What would you do if someone were here?

"Hello?" She tiptoed from bathroom, through the bedroom, to the living room, to the kitchen, then back to the living room, holding the towel around her. The layout was the same as her apartment.

Velma peeked out the front door into the hall. The door had a gold H on it, her apartment letter.

This is beyond weird. Are you in the wrong building? These complexes look so much alike. No, that couldn't be. Be real. Your key let you in the building, opened this door.

She closed the door, not sure what to do. None of this was plausible. Yet, she was stuck in a strange apartment with no clothes. What if someone came in? She sat on the edge of an unfamiliar living-room chair.

Think. You came home upset at what you'd done. You went right to the bedroom, dropped your purse and briefcase on the floor, yanked off your clothes as you moved to the bathroom, then jumped in the shower. You didn't really look around the apartment, but certainly you would have noticed you were in the wrong place, wouldn't you?

Nothing made sense. Velma looked around the living room. The furnishings were not to her taste. The sofa and two chairs had large yellow flower patterns against dark green. A cheap reproduction of Monet's arched bridge in his Giverny gardens curled out from a chipped plastic frame hanging at a tilt above the phone. Why don't people just buy original art? Good art's not that expensive.

Oh, god, listen to you. Pay attention. The wet towel is soaking through the chair. Get dressed.

She got up and went back to the bedroom. Her things definitely were not where she'd left them. But who could have taken them? Did someone come in, hear her in the shower, and take her clothes? Why would they do that? Maybe they went to get the police. God, what a mess. Now she'd have to get a new driver's license, credit cards, checkbook, everything.

Why are you thinking about that stuff? You don't even know where you are—wherever here is. Don't you think that's a little more important? What are you going to do?

Velma stared at herself in the large mirror that covered the sliding closet door. She saw her short red hair, green eyes now red from crying before, her furrowed brow, straight nose and thin lips. The wrinkle cream wasn't doing a lot of good, though. Her figure wasn't bad for her age. But the Stairmaster wasn't doing much for the cellulite on her thighs. Did he notice? How could he not have!

Are you so needy that you'd use a student? That's what you did, you know.

Velma slid the mirrored door away from her, revealing a woman's wardrobe. Dresses, skirts, blouses, coats, shoes. None of them hers. But sizes, she discovered, fit her, even though she saw nothing to her taste.

You'd better put something on. You can't stand around naked. Try those jeans and that green blouse. You need a bra. You're starting to sag. No, forget it. You'd better not look through the dresser drawers. You've already gone a bit far just being here.

Velma dressed, wanting the clothes to cover her shame. What must the student be thinking about now? Was he as self-condemning as she? Did he have regrets? Did he enjoy it? Was he bragging to friends? Telling them of his conquest? Who used whom?

You'd better be thinking about why you're in some strange apartment taking a shower and borrowing clothes. The police could come banging on the door any minute asking what you're doing here.

Velma threw herself on the bed. This can't be happening! I don't understand! What's going on? Why? Why me?

Perhaps you're being punished.

Punished? By whom?

You should know. You studied psychology. You know you should have been less impulsive, thought ahead better. Too hasty to fulfill that pudding craving. Wondering if it was worth the complications. Too late now. Get up, find out where you are, and get out of here.

Velma slipped on a pair of sandals from the closet. Heading for the door to leave, she passed the vagina-like flower on the wall. A Georgia O'Keeffe reproduction? What happened to Monet's arched bridge? She looked around but no Monet hung on any wall.

You'd better get out of here. You're starting to hallucinate.

She tried, but the door wouldn't open. Velma turned the knob every which way, tugged, yanked, pounded, everything. But the door wouldn't budge.

You opened it before. Try again.

The door would not open.

Velma pounded on the door, yelling, "What's going on? Who's doing this? Somebody answer me! Let me out of here!"

She went to a window and tried to open it, but she couldn't get it to move.

What good would that do, anyway? You're six stories up.

Maybe someone would hear me. Across the way, in the next building, a sign in a window read, "THE TRUTH IS NOT HERE."

The phone rang. Velma jumped, turned. Her moist, frightened eyes held the phone as it rang—stopped—rang—stopped —rang—beckoning.

Answer it.

No. It couldn't be for her. This isn't her place.

But maybe the person calling could help with some answers. Answer it. It seems it's not going to stop until you do.

"Hello?"

She heard someone sigh, then Carly Simon began singing, "My romance, doesn't need a castle rising in Spain…"

"Who is this?"

"My romance, doesn't need…"

Velma slammed the receiver in its cradle. She looked at her shaking hands, felt the shock spread through her, jumped when the phone rang again, sat staring at the phone while it rang and rang and rang.

Don't answer it.

The phone stopped ringing, then came a click, a red light flashed and a mechanical voice on the answering machine tape began: "Hester Prynne, Anna Karenina, Emma Bovary, Donna Rice, Kelly Flinn, e tu Velma?"

"Stop it! Stop it!" Velma grabbed the answering machine, pulled the cord, and threw it against the Van Gogh self-portrait with the bandage over his ear, knocking it from the wall and ripping one corner loose from the frame. The machine's red light kept blinking.

Velma buried her face in her hands, weeping. How can this be happening? Who's doing this? What do they want? I admit I was wrong. Bad professional behavior. Self-indulgent. I seduced him. I abused my position. I shouldn't have. Velma sank to the floor. "But men…my male colleagues…they do it all the time."

You think that excuses your behavior?

No, no. I—I was swept away. An uncontrollable passion. He was, too. I think. We were going over his paper, a very intelligent one on the way the hypothalamus directs the pituitary, which in turn directs the gonads to secrete the sex hormones, when it just— happened. We looked at each other. Before we knew it… oh, I can't explain. I can't even believe it.

Right there in your office.

Yes.

On the floor.

Yes.

You can't call it love.

Oh, god, no. Not even romance.

You can't call it adultery, either. Neither one of you is married.

Lust. Just plain animal lust. Lust over responsibility.

He's not a minor, is he?"

No. He's probably twenty-two or twenty-three.

You'd better hope so. And you'd better hope he isn't HIV positive or carrying some disease like herpes or gonorrhea.

A loud, droning buzz from the bedroom pierced Velma's ears, softened some, then persisted. She knew she had to…no… was expected to go look. She tiptoed past the reproduction she'd knocked to the floor, Judith Bernstein's Cockman#1, and peered around the bedroom door. The irritating sound came from a radio by the bed.

She pushed the off button and heard her own voice come from the radio, repeating: Wash—him—off. Wash—him—off.

Velma screamed, ran to the bathroom, dropping her borrowed clothes on the floor, and slammed the shower door behind her.

STUDENT TEACHER

Beat her? No. Never.

Hit her? Mm. Yes. Once, sad to say. Just once, though. Slapped her face before I'd realized it.

Oh, she was probably about sixteen then.

I don't dwell on it, no, but yes, I think about it sometimes. Not proudly.

Regret, actually.

Yes, well, you're digging up ancient history here.

Okay. Let's see. I was still teaching at the college. Teaching *Huck Finn*, ironically. I remember, because what happened made me internalize that book. A personal epiphany, you could say. More personal than I could ever make it for my students, that's for sure.

Anyway, one night my son Brian—he's the youngest—about thirteen at the time—knocked on our bedroom door, woke me up, and told us that Teri had slipped...

Yes, my daughter—had slipped out her bedroom window and gone off with some boy on his motorcycle. Poor guy didn't want to be a snitch, but he was worried about his sister running off like that. Thought maybe she'd run away because he knew Teri was upset.

No, she'd never done any thing like that before. Surprised me.

You know, I honestly can't remember what prompted it. She and my husband had had words earlier. Got sent to her room for some reason. I can't remember why.

No, it wasn't unusual for them. Once Teri hit fourteen, it seemed like they couldn't agree on anything. I got stuck in the middle a lot. Seemed like my husband was always finding fault with Teri. Felt she couldn't do anything right.

Me? I never knew whose side I was supposed to take. I didn't like having to deal with all that arguing. I don't know. Sometimes— sometimes it seemed my husband was—oh, I don't know. Hard to explain. It all made me uncomfortable.

Whose side? Well, my husband's, I guess.

Good question. I—I don't know why.

Afraid of him? No. I mean—afraid? I never thought so. Anyway, what could I have done?

I see what you mean. Guess I should have been more of an arbitrator, tried to see Teri's side better.

My husband? Yeah, he drinks pretty heavily sometimes. Of course, he doesn't think so. But he often doesn't remember what he said or did the next day, even after two or three drinks.

Well, yes, to be honest, he does embarrass me. I mean, he gets glassy-eyed, says stupid things, flirts with my women colleagues…

Don't think so. I mean, I never saw him hit Teri.

Sure. Well, after Brian woke me up, I shook my husband, but it was impossible to wake him. We'd had some people over that night for dinner and he'd put away more than his share of drinks. I sent Brian back to bed and told him not to worry, but actually I was shaken. I mean, Teri's the oldest, so raising a teenage girl for the first time, well, I didn't know how to handle something like this, you know?

Feelings? You name it. Mostly anger at first. Angry that she'd sneaked off, disobeyed—angry to be awakened—angry that I had to deal with this alone while my husband snored on—angry at him for making Teri upset so much—angry I'd be in lousy shape to teach in the morning…

Of course, fear, yes. Worried with fear that something ugly might happen to Teri—an accident on a motorcycle—a call from the police—fear she'd become a runaway picture on a milk carton—get pregnant by some weirdo kid I didn't know. I didn't know any of her friends rode motorcycles. Mostly I didn't know what to do. I couldn't sleep—it was one o'clock in the morning. I had no idea where she went or with whom. All I could do was wait until she returned—if she returned. Of course, the more time went by the more I became pissed at my husband lying there oblivious to it all. I tried shaking him, telling him to wake up, share the misery, but he just muttered gibberish. God, he made me furious, so furious…

What? Oh, sorry. Didn't realize I'd stopped.

What did I do? Well, for a while I went downstairs and walked around the house in the dark. I tried watching television, but even with all those channels there was nothing that could interest me. I tried grading some test papers, but that was impossible. Mostly I just sat in a chair in the dark.

Finally, going on three o'clock, I heard Teri coming back in through the window, so I rushed up the stairs to her room and flicked the light switch. She just looked at me like the clichéd deer frozen in the on-coming headlights. Neither of us said anything at first. Then I blurted out the parental "just-what-do-you-think-you're-doing" and "where-have-you-been" and "who-were-you-with" stuff. Soap opera classic, you know.

Nothing. She just looked at me and said nothing. I yelled at her to answer me, but she just looked at me. For the first time, I noticed how much she looked like my husband. That's when I slapped her across the face. Oh, god, I was enraged. Then she said—I'll never forget her words—"If that makes you feel good, why don't you hit me again." I drew my arm back, wanting to.

No. I don't know what stopped me. Saw myself, I guess—what I was doing. My arm fell limp. I sank down on her bed, dizzy from it all. It suddenly didn't feel like I was living *my* life, you know? I mean, this whole scene was out of some insipid story or sitcom. Yet there I was, a major character yelling at my own daughter—*slapping* her for god's sake. Then she really surprised me.

It was what she said. She said, very calmly, "You're such a hypocrite."

I was stunned.

Why? Because she took me aback, given the context. She was the one I thought had done wrong and should be punished, but here she was calling me a hypocrite, looking at me like I was the guilty one.

You bet I felt confused. She stood looking down at me sitting there on the bed and let loose. She had overheard me talking with the dinner guests about how I enjoyed teaching *Huck Finn*, how I admired Huck, his independence, his unwillingness to be "sivilized" according to the Widow Douglas and her sister Miss Watson, his decision to go to hell if need be rather than turn Jim in. Somehow she saw herself as Huck and my husband and I were the widow and her sister. We were trying to civilize her according to our rules, rules she felt were sometimes unfair. I mean, this was a teenager's logic, but still…

Suddenly, I found myself the student and her the teacher. She began crying as she spoke, saying we didn't like her, thought she never did anything right, always grounded her before ever hearing her side, never giving her any credit, restricting her freedom from learning about life and people on her own. I never stood up for her, she said. I always went along with her father. Couldn't I see how he dominated both of us? Both of us. She said she'd sneaked out her window—just like Huck, she reminded me—because she needed to get out and talk to someone about us. So she'd called the boy on the motorcycle to come get her.

Why him? Because they were good friends at school, she said. Someone she could talk to. She'd been afraid to introduce him because she knew her father wouldn't like him or his motorcycle— and she thought I'd probably just agree.

Yes, I later met him. Name's Wes. Seems like a nice enough kid.

No, she assured me, theirs was not a sexual relationship. Wes was a good listener, she said. He helped calm her down when she got mad at us. He's the one who insisted she come home.

Was she right? You mean, about the way we treated her?

Well, I can see now she was right about a lot of it. I just never looked at what went on from her perspective.

I felt so bad I got up and held her while she sobbed. I was surprised at how tall she'd grown. It had been a long time, too long, since I had hugged her, or consoled her, or even really listened to her. Where had I been?

Then came my own tears. That's when I knew.

It wasn't really Teri I'd slapped.

"**D**amn."

Why hadn't she written it down? She even kept a pad and pencil by her bedside, like every writer's manual and workshop suggests. As she lay in bed last night, she'd come up with the perfect opening line, a sure-fire reader grabber, words she was sure she'd remember this morning. Gone now.

The cursor on her blank monitor kept blinking what her mind was thinking: stu—pid—stu—pid—stu—pid.

She'd become that Kudzu cartoon character sitting at his computer with a blank dialogue bubble over his head.

She sipped her coffee. "Yuk." Cold as her brain. She leaned back in her chair, which tilted more than she expected, and spilled coffee in her lap causing her to jerk forward, spilling more coffee between her legs, on the chair, and on the carpet.

"Dammit!"

Now she had to go to the kitchen for a rag to clean up. She'd never get anything written at this rate.

Once in the kitchen, her wired-hair terrier penned up in the adjoining laundry room began barking. She knew that meant, "Take me out, or I'll flood the floor."

"Okay, Okay. Just a minute, Pulitzer."

She wet a clean rag, dabbed at the coffee on her dark sweat pants, then went back to her desk and tried to clean up the coffee stains.

"Jeez! These stains'll never come out." At least she hadn't spilled coffee on her keyboard.

She went back to Pulitzer, pulled back the small gate she had installed to keep the dog out of the kitchen area and groaned.

"Oh, god, Pulitzer! Look what you've done!"

The floor looked like two inches of powdered snow had fallen. A giant-sized box of laundry soap had been chewed to pieces. Pulitzer sat there with a soap flake smile in his whiskers, his tail brushing against the floor like a short windshield wiper.

"Dammit, Pulitzer!"

Misunderstanding her tone, the dog jumped up ready for attention. His front paws, clogged with soap powder, clawed against her damp sweat pants, leaving streaks of white against dark blue. Instinctively, she jumped back, allowing the dog an escape into the kitchen area. Pulitzer, overjoyed at being loose, ran around the kitchen, shaking soap powder off his body, and leaving little patches of white here and there.

"No, Pulitzer! Bad dog! Get back here! Oh, god!"

She grabbed the leash from the back-door hook and, after some chasing, caught Pulitzer by his collar. The dog decided to turn the hooking of the leash into a wiggling game, forcing her to tug and turn in circles. When she opened the back door, Pulitzer raced between her legs, dragging the leash behind him.

"Pulitzer! Come back here!"

Pulitzer stopped at the trashcan, lifted a rear leg, and let go a full bladder.

"Oh, real nice. Couldn't you at least have waited until we got to the lawn?"

When finished, Pulitzer jumped into her geranium bed, turned in a couple of circles, then let go with his bowels.

"Pulitzer! Bad dog!" She stood there feeling foolish, watching. Pulitzer's look implied she should look the other way.

His business finished, Pulitzer kicked his back legs in an attempt to cover up what he'd done, uprooting a couple of geraniums.

"Pulitzer!" She grabbed the dog's leash.

Ignoring her, he strained against the leash and headed for the street.

"Okay, okay. We'll walk. Maybe my writing muse will be waiting for me when we get back." She let Pulitzer lead her on their usual neighborhood route.

About a block down the street, Pulitzer pulled her toward a yard with a chain link fence. A black lab behind the fence gave a bark then wagged a welcome for Pulitzer as he stuck his nose through one of the links.

Okay, reader, stop! Hold it right here. This story's going nowhere, and it won't as long as we're stuck in Helen's point of view (notice her name's not even mentioned before I jumped in). Think about it. What's happened so far? Helen can't remember something she should have written down, she's spilled coffee, half-assed cleaned it up, barked at me for doing dog things, and now she's taking me for a walk. That's a story? And what's going to happen when we get back? Clean up my mess. Oh, my. Won't that be exciting.

See, Helen has this idea she's going to write the great American novel. Yeah, sure, along with a thousand other frustrated literature teachers. I don't mean to badmouth her. Helen's good to me, a nice lady and all that, but you know what her chances are. More people are writing than reading these days.

Not like the old days. Writing was a craft at worst, an art at best. Sure, junk got published, too, but publishers looked for quality, had editors work with authors, and helped develop talent. But now it's corporation buy-out time. All the publishing houses want is the big blockbuster, the moneymakers with movies and television tie-ins, not quality stuff or even pretty good stuff. Writers like Helen haven't got a prayer, no room in the inn. She should stick to teaching.

How do I know? Past lives.

I'm known in certain circles as a literary hound. Way back, I've lost track how far back, I committed some big sin I won't get into now, but I'm stuck in something like my own Dante's Inferno. Until I do something to redeem myself, I'm stuck being some writer's dog in each of my lives. Right now it's Helen I get, but

I've been around with some of the greats—Homer (she was black, you know), Dante (now there's an imagination), Chaucer (a kick), Tolstoy (heavy dude, let me tell you), Melville, Twain, Austin, both Brontës (fought like cats), Faulkner, Hemingway (jeez, those two put the sauce away), and…

Sorry, now I'm off on a tangent, and that doesn't make for a good story either. But trust me here, and see if things don't develop a little better if we get out of Helen's point of view. Sure, it's against all the textbook rules to change the point of view in a story, but come on, dear reader, the change is for the better. See if you don't agree.

Pulitzer makes Helen stop at Dickens' place every day. Dickens is the black lab mentioned in that other point of view. Helen doesn't know it. How could she? But part of Pulitzer's redemption task is to communicate with other dogs, tell them stories that help them evolve their karma so they don't get eternally stuck as a literary hound, the pits for a dog.

"Morning, Pulitzer," Dickens barks. "You're early today."

"Morning, Dick. Yeah, I had to get Helen out of the house. She's struggling with her writing again."

"What's her problem this time?"

"Same old, same old. False starts. Thinks she's got something to say that's entertaining and morally uplifting."

"How long has she been working on that novel, anyway?"

"Three years. Just before she got me. Sad to watch, I'll tell you." Pulitzer sniffed along the fence. "Hey, some new dog's been here since yesterday."

Dickens sat and put his nose part way through one of the chain links. "Yeah. New bitch two blocks up. Irish wolfhound, I think."

"Something familiar about that odor." Pulitzer sniffed around some more. "Wolfhound, huh." Pulitzer lifted his leg, dribbled a bit, then put his nose close to Dickens's. They both lay down facing each other. "I'll lead Helen up there and check her out."

"Lucky you. I haven't been out of this yard for two weeks. I'm about ready to jump the fence and roam around a while. It's a bleak house around here these days." Dickens scratched an itch behind his ear. "Mr. Copperfield's come on hard times."

"Sorry to hear that, Dick. But take my advice. Don't jump. Stay put. It might feel good to be loose for a while, but you'll end up homeless, or in the pound, or squashed flat by a speeder. It's not safe for dogs here in Dorrit. Town's gotten too big." Pulitzer snipped at a flea crawling across his belly. "Be glad you're not a lit hound."

"You're probably right. And I did hear Copperfield say he had some great expectations, something about a big happening in two cities."

"Yeah, well, hang in there. Gotta move on. Maybe see you on the way back." Pulitzer got up.

"Probably won't. I'm going in and try to console Mr. Copperfield. He likes it when I sit by him, lick his hand, stick my head in his lap, stuff like that."

"Take it from one who knows. Do your assigned job right. You'll be rewarded for that down the line. See ya."

The new scent got stronger as Pulitzer led Helen up the street. The closer they got, the harder Pulitzer pulled, anxious to see the new dog.

Then there she was, on the front porch of her new home, an albino Irish wolfhound, rolled on her side looking bored. Pulitzer stopped. His body went stiff, and then began trembling.

He felt Helen trying to coax him on. "Come on, boy, that one's too big for you."

But Pulitzer held firm against the leash and barked, "Molly! Is that you, Molly?"

The wolfhound's ears twitched. She stretched her neck, trying not to appear too interested. She stared at Pulitzer, then sat up letting out an odd yelp.

"Saints preserve us! Blazes, is it really you now?"

Pulitzer's wagging tail shook his rear end. "'Tis, Molly. Only me name's Pulitzer this time 'round."

"Pulitzer, is it? Well, you'll always be Blazes to me, you little scamp." Molly got up on all fours and came down the steps, then stopped. "I can get no closer, Blazes. Hooked up I am with an electronic fence. Another step and I get a shock that sends me ten feet nearer heaven."

"Not to worry." Pulitzer tugged with all his might, catching Helen off guard and managed to reach Molly, where the two of them nosed around in friendly tail wagging re-acquaintance.

Pulitzer felt Helen yank on the leash and dragged him back a few feet. "Dammit, Pulitzer. We don't know these people. They're new here. They may not like us in their yard."

Molly growled and barked, frightening Helen, who dropped the leash and ran back to the sidewalk.

While Helen yelled at Pulitzer to come, boy, Pulitzer thanked Molly. "That should keep her busy for a few minutes. Dog-gone, it's good to see you. I haven't seen you since Dublin. What's brought you to Dorrit?"

"I'm on Episode Seventeen, Blazes. One more author to go and I'm through."

"Seventeen, huh. That's grand, Molly. Why, you were only on Four when I lived with Joyce." Pulitzer moved further away from Helen so she couldn't get his leash without getting closer to Molly.

"And you, Blazes?" Molly inquired. "Aren't you close to being through?"

"No." He reached his front legs out and then arched in a stretch. "Had a wee bit of trouble on Six. Got put back to Episode One.

"Oh, dear. She's a beginner then." Molly tossed her head toward Helen.

Pulitzer nodded. "Plus, I have to redeem myself before I can move up."

"Jesus, Mary and Joseph! What'd you do to deserve all that?"

"Aw, 'tis a stupid thing, really. Remember those schema chart things Joyce did for that book he was writing?"

"The big fat rambling thing he called his Homeric parallel?"

"The same. Well, the family readied to move to Switzerland and they were going to leave me behind. I went a bit mad. Chewed up his schemas."

"Blazes! You didn't!"

"Did."

Helen appeared to be coming closer, still calling out "Come on, boy. Let's go now." So Molly stepped forward, shook her massive body and barked. Helen stepped back again.

"Still, the man finished his book." Molly offered.

"He did, indeed. A great classic, some think. Not many ever finish reading it though." Pulitzer tried to catch a flea running up one leg. "Personally, I think destroying those papers forced him to write a better book. But the powers that be claim I kept the man from writing more than he did. So here I am."

"Anything I can do to help?"

"Naw, but thanks. I got me self in trouble, up to me now."

"Pulitzer, dammit, get over here right now!" Helen stamped her foot, close to tears.

"Look, I have to go. Helen's gonna have cats if I don't get back to her. It's grand to know you're in the neighborhood. I'll see you tomorrow and we'll talk more."

"Things are looking up, knowing you're around, Blazes—or shall I call you Pulitzer?"

"A rose by any other name…" Pulitzer called back as he went to Helen.

Helen grabbed his leash, scolding and wagging her finger at him. "You're a naughty dog. What's with you? You must learn to come when I call you."

Pulitzer yawned and tuned her out, thinking about Molly and the old days. She'd done all right by herself. Only one more Episode and she'd be through.

"Well," he told himself, "you have your hands full with Helen. Deal with that. One Episode at a time."

Wasn't that better? Now, let's mix the points of view and see what happens.

The following day, Pulitzer and Helen met Molly and her owner on their walk. Pulitzer had Molly deliberately entangle their leashes so their owners would have to engage in conversation.

Helen felt embarrassed, not sure how to begin untangling the mess.

Helen's frustration with the leashes amused Molly.

"Nice, your man?" Pulitzer asked, also amused.

"Very. And single. Quite a fine writer. Two novels out." Molly added, "But trouble he's having finishing his third right now."

Pulitzer looked at Helen, then at the man. "Hm. You know, Molly, they could use each other. She can't begin; he can't finish."

Helen gave up on the leashes and looked to Molly's owner for help. "I'm so sorry about this. The two met yesterday when we walked by your place. Pulitzer took a liking to your dog right away. I had trouble getting him back. She's quite beautiful."

"Yes, isn't she. You don't see many albino wolfhounds." He paused looking at Molly, then looked at Helen and extended a hand. "I'm Adam Ribb, by the way. And you're…?"

"You may be right, Blazes," Molly said.

"Would you look at the way they're eye-balling each other. Oh, there's interest there. Okay, Helen, don't be stupid. Do it right."

"Adam Ribb. Not the writer?" Helen asked, no longer interested in the leashes, which had now entwined the four of them together.

"Oh, you've read me?" Adam looked a bit embarrassed.

"Both your books. Loved them. Can't wait for the next one. You're writing a trilogy, I read somewhere."

"Let's keep them wrapped up as long as we can," Blazes suggested. "Let 'em get a good whiff of each other."

See how that worked? Let's try a more omniscient point of view now.

And a good whiff they got. After a time, the four were untangled and went their separate ways. But not until Helen and Adam had recognized their shared literary interests and made a date for coffee the next morning.

The four met at Java Jitters, a quiet place and safe for a first meeting where Helen and Adam discussed writing. Adam brought parts of his manuscript in trouble and read some passages to Helen. Since Helen had read his other two books, understood the complexities of writing, and taught literature, Adam respected her opinions and any advice she offered.

Pulitzer and Molly, comfortably tied up under a tree outside the coffee house, reminisced over past Episodes. Molly, Pulitzer learned, had completed Episodes with Kafka, Ibsen, Strindberg, and Wharton. Pulitzer felt the less said about his exploits the better.

After drinking more coffee than they normally do, Helen and Adam left Java Jitters for home. Crossing a street, the pair was so engaged in conversation that neither noticed when they reached the other side that pages of Adam's manuscript had slipped from his folder leaving a paper trail in the crosswalk.

Pulitzer noticed. Yanking loose from Helen, he ran back into the street and sat by the pages barking for attention.

The other three turned in time to see a screeching car hit Pulitzer and knock him in the air. He landed on his back.

Molly yelped and began jumping about. Helen and Adam ran to Pulitzer. The driver approached them. "I didn't see him until too late. He ran in front of me and sat down. I couldn't stop. I'm so sorry."

Pulitzer tried to get up, one leg twitching, but after a weak effort, lay still.

Here's a good place for Pulitzer's viewpoint.

Pulitzer, aware that people were standing about him, thought he heard Molly's whining and Helen's crying. He wanted to tell them he was okay, to pick up Adam's pages before they blew away, that's what this was all about. But he had no voice. And their voices seemed to be fading, their bodies growing distant. Then he knew what was happening, and the future touched him.

Helen, in her grief, would write about him in a story that would begin her career as a short story writer. She'd never write the great American novel, but she'd make a recognized literary name for herself within the academic community. She and Adam would collaborate later. Pulitzer felt good as his point of view dissolved into a blinding white something or other.

"Damn."

He could kick himself for not having written it down last night. He even kept a pen and pad on his night table. But he'd been so sure he'd remember it this morning he hadn't bothered. The words, so easily flowing in bed last night, were now gone.

The cursor on his monitor blinked what his mind was thinking: fool—ish—fool—ish—fool—ish.

He remembered that Kudzu cartoon, the one with the writer sitting at his computer under a blank dialogue bubble. It fit him. Nothing was coming out right.

Taking a sip of coffee now as cold as his creativity, he leaned back in his chair, which tilted more than he expected, and spilled coffee down his shirt and in his lap causing him to jerk forward, spilling more coffee between his legs, on the chair, and on the carpet.

"Dammit!"

Now he had to go to the kitchen for a rag to clean up. Hell, he'd never get anything written at this rate.

Once in the kitchen, his golden retriever penned up in the adjoining laundry room, began barking. He knew that meant, "Take me out. It's time for a walk."

"Okay, Hemingway, old boy. Hang on. My mess comes first."

Hemingway wagged his tail, eager for Episode Two.

"**D**id you do that?"
"What?"
"You know."
Not looking up from the student's mid-term test he was grading, George took his time answering. "No."
"Now, George, you know you did. Why don't you just say so?"
His teeth clenched from that I-know-I'm-right tone Hannah sometimes used. He knew she hated it when he wouldn't admit to something she thought he did. He also knew she wouldn't let up until she had proven herself right.
"Okay, okay, I did it. Satisfied?" His irritation struck more at himself than her, really. It wasn't like he did it on purpose. But lately, well, he lacked control sometimes. And in more ways than one.
"Really, George, I don't see why you bother to deny it. Why did you deny it?"
"Why do you even need to ask? Only two of us in this room that I can see."
He didn't mean to sound so harsh, but he didn't know why himself. Self-denial? Angry at his growing loss of control? Growing older? Who knows? Anyway, he wasn't trying to be mean. Yet, he found himself peeving Hannah lately, almost enjoying it. Silly. Childish.

"Well, yes, but you didn't have to deny it." He caught Hannah's stretching of the word to emphasize his transgression. "It's quite natural, after all. It just…"

George knew the pause meant she was searching for just the right words.

"Well, it's, you know, the odor, that's all." He watched her chin dip and peek at him over the top of her glasses, embarrassed.

George couldn't help himself. "Now, since you seem to be an authority on the subject, allow me to add to your knowledge. You do it more when you get older. That's a fact."

"Speak for yourself." Her eyes quickly left him for her magazine.

"I am. Who else could I speak for? The older I get the more I do it—absolutely uncontrollable sometimes. I'm a living example."

"Well, that's enough on the subject." Hannah squirmed in her chair. "Let's discuss something else," she said in a manner that prompted George to continue.

"Broccoli makes the worst ones." He peeked her way. "Speaking for myself, of course."

Hannah remained silent. George watched her push her glasses further up the bridge of her nose and stare into her magazine, indicating that as far as she was concerned she wished no further discussion on the topic.

"There's that old culprit cauliflower, too," George went on, watching her on the sly. "But broccoli seems to be the worst offender. Speaking for myself, that is."

Hannah raised her chin a bit but kept her eyes on the magazine George knew she couldn't possibly be reading now. He had her.

"Some people say cheese does it to them. Not me, though. Little ones from white cheese maybe. Then there's…"

"George! Now that's enough!" Hannah snapped her magazine to her lap.

"What makes you do it the most, hon?" George asked, eyes trying innocence, a slight, pursed smile she couldn't see.

"George! What's gotten into you?"

"Well, after all these years, I don't see any harm in telling me, since we're on the subject." He tried to look as virtuous as possible.

"If you want to talk, let's talk about something more interesting."

"This is interesting. I'd really like to know."

"I hate that—that word and see no reason for this discussion."

George smiled inside as Hannah scowled at him, raised herself from the chair, smoothed out her skirt underneath her, and sat back down. He knew she was turning pages in her magazine too quickly to be seeing anything.

He couldn't help himself and went on. "Well, you do it, too. Don't deny it. And some are pretty powerful. I should know after thirty-four years. Anyway, you already admitted it was natural." He tried to sound a bit hurt at her reluctance to engage in a discussion.

"Well, it is, but that doesn't mean I want to talk about—it."

"You mean passing gas? Breaking wind? Parting the waves? Cutting cheese? Slicing the icing?"

"Now, George, just stop it. I don't know what's going on with you lately. You're acting so—so strange. You scare me. It's like suddenly living with a different man. Do you feel all right? Is there something the matter, something you're not telling me?"

George nodded his head, put the student test back on the class stack of papers on the reading table and placed his reading glasses on top. He knew he would no longer be able to grade fairly tonight. He rubbed the bridge of his nose and closed his eyes.

"I called one of my students a lying little twit today."

"George, you didn't. To her face?"

He nodded twice, then his head dropped back, tilting toward one shoulder. He rubbed the palms of his hands over his face.

"You're not saying this to get a rise out of me, now, are you, George?"

"No." He took a deep breath. "No, she just got to me with all her damned excuses, you know? I mean, she misses class all the time, comes late often when she does come. Always fooling with her cell phone. Her last report was plagiarized. Took it right off that new computer program in the library. Then tried to lie about that. She called me mean, I called her a lying little twit, and told her to get out of my office."

"Oh, George."

George knew by the way Hannah said his name that she wanted to hold his head in her lap and scratch him behind the ears. He probably reminded her of the way their old dog Scooter looked when he got scolded.

"It's been a tough year." His voice cracked. "Very tough. Things just aren't the same, Hannah."

For years the classroom had been his life, his love, his students his second family. Oh, he and Hannah had raised two fine, successful children of their own. He'd felt he'd been a loving father and husband. But in a way he felt he led two lives. He'd never shared that feeling with Hannah. Too private, too hard to explain. Besides, he feared she'd never understand if he tried.

But this year, something felt wrong. He didn't feel secure there anymore. The pleasure he'd always felt in teaching, his comfort and familiarity with the classroom—all that had slipped off somewhere. He'd always taken pride in his ability to get students interested in what he was teaching, to watch their enthusiasm grow. But of late, they didn't seem to care, their heads down playing with their cell phones. Now he found himself losing patience with his students, a growing intolerance toward them. He'd never called a student a twit or any other name before. Now it surprised him sometimes at what slipped out of his mouth—and other parts of his anatomy.

"Maybe," Hannah broke into his thoughts, "well, dear, maybe you should retire."

"Retire? Why do you think I should retire?" George, uneasy at the thought, got up and moved to the window, a long, overt act of flatulence trailing him.

"George!"

"Couldn't help it, dammit. Told you—uncontrollable sometimes, just slips out." He stared out the window, but only saw yesterday.

"I was standing in line at the bank and out one slips nice as you please. Little teenage prick behind me starts laughing. People looking, smiling. Me, trying to pretend it didn't matter while my face burned hot. Didn't smell, thank god. Just a noise, but talk about embarrassed. The distinguished philosophy professor. Ha! Jeez."

"Well, it happens to everybody."

"Did it ever happen to you?"

"No, but…"

"I think it only happens to older men," George reflected pensively. "I remember my dad used to do it a lot when he got older. After a while he'd do it right in front of you and act like it never happened. I never heard him use the word 'fart,' though, you know? Always said 'break wind.' My mother, too. Now everybody can say fart, shit, piss, fuck—nobody cares."

"Well, I certainly care. I don't want you to speak like that around me. You never have and I hope you never will."

"That's part of what's wrong with this world, you know. Everybody's too open. Nothing is private. We've gone overboard. Why, look at the newspapers and TV news. They're full of nothing but items about wives whacking off their husband's penis…"

"George!"

"…the latest celebrity to come out of the closet, who's got the most money, everyone's' sex life exposed, in detail, gets front page space. I bet if the president farted in front of a reporter that would make the headlines. There'd probably be a sound bite on TV. Then the pundits would analyze it for its political potency. No, not like the old days. Nope. Huh-un."

"Maybe you should see the doctor, George. I don't know what it is, but something's wrong. You don't seem happy anymore. You come home complaining about things at school. That's not at all like you. Are you sure you're not keeping something from me? Are you feeling ill?"

"You know," George went on not hearing, "when I first started teaching, you never heard a student curse in class. They were polite. They knew certain words were just not to be used. But the last few years? My god! The word 'fuck' has become a classroom standby. Remember, I told you about that student who told me to 'fuck off'? And nobody thought a thing of it. Standard procedure for talking to an instructor."

George walked around the room, then sat down across from Hannah.

Hannah made an unthinking face, covered her nose with her hand, and eyed George.

George sighed, "Yes, it was me—again." Then he grinned. "It really is the quiet ones that stink, isn't it? When I was a kid we always accused the one who said they didn't smell anything. 'Eeyoo, you don't smell that? Then it must be you!' Usually true, too."

"George, I'm really worried about you."

"Well, light a match. Burn incense."

"That's not what I mean."

"I know. I know." He sighed, eyes staring at the floor, seeing nothing. "Truth is, so am I. Lately I've been doing it in class a lot. Mostly just little noises I don't think anybody's noticed. But I'll be walking down the hall to class and, ffffft, out one pops. It gets lost in the crowd, thank god. Or standing at the urinal—ffft. Uncontrollable. Sooner or later it's bound to happen, you know. Image me standing in front of my class expounding on Nietzsche's belief that life is essentially a will to power, the feeling that one is in command of oneself, when I—with no control—let one."

He ran a little movie in his head seeing himself farting in front of his class, students pointing, laughing, him standing there totally humiliated, destroyed, forever remembered as that senile old fart.

"What a legacy after thirty-eight years of teaching philosophy. 'The old fart.' No distinguished professor emeritus for me. No way."

"Oh, George."

"I don't know, Hannah. It's not just the farts. There's that waking pressure and urinating ten times during a night, and creaking body joints, ugly hairs growing out my ears and nose, triple chins looking back at me in the mirror, thinning, gray hair, just plain old."

"Sixty-five's not old," Hannah consoled, "not these days."

"Christ, I look at my students, and they're so young. I never used to feel a distance, you know? I always felt connected to them, like a unit. But now I don't connect with them like I used to. I'm not a part of them any more—their music, their clothes, their tattoos, their body piercing, their skateboards. Their cell phones interrupt my lectures. Even their language. Why, the word 'said' has all but disappeared. Now it's 'and he goes blah, blah, blah; and she goes blah, blah, blah.' And the word *like* punctuates every other word. 'Sir, do we, like, need to know that for the test? Like, is this really like important to know?' I don't know, Hannah, I just don't know."

George looked at Hannah and his eyes clouded. He hid his head in his hands.

Hannah went to him and touched his thinning hair. "Come on, you're a great teacher, George, and you know it. Your students have always thought highly of you. Your evaluations are always excellent."

He took her hands in his, kissed the tips of her fingers, and turned his head away.

He hadn't told her about the latest ones. They weren't bad, but they weren't up to his usual standards for himself. Before, he'd always felt that his students liked him; some, he felt, well, maybe even loved him in that teacher-student kind of feeling. He certainly had loved many of them. Some he had loved like a son or daughter. Some he had loved for their brains, some for their humor, some for their tenacity to learn, and some of the young women for their bodies. Oh, god, some of those bodies. Yes, he admitted it. Never shared that with any one, but, yes, over the years he had fantasized about some, like Carter, lusted in silence after others. Well, he was human, after all. Still, he'd never taken advantage of his position, even those times when he knew in his gut that his advances would have been accepted. Certainly, many of his colleagues had and still did use their position, but he never did. Even though there were times…well…

No, it wouldn't have been right. He'd always loved teaching because he'd really loved his students, respected them, wanted to help them. Back in the early days, he used to tell friends he felt guilty getting paid for teaching. Of course, the pay wasn't much, laughable even, but he discovered he was successful and respected, because he loved his students and tried his best to guide them to be successful. He'd get angry with those teachers who always complained about their students, calling them brainless Neanderthals and worse. He always wondered why they kept on teaching if they hated their classes so much. He told himself that if he ever felt that way, he'd quit teaching.

Maybe he should retire. Now he was calling his students little twits and pricks and thinking worse. Besides, what did he have to show for nearly forty years of giving his life to educate others? If he'd been a musician, an artist, a writer, he'd have works to show for it, tangible accomplishments others could share and enjoy. If he'd been an architect or a contractor, he could point to a building and say, "Yes, I did that." If he'd been a scientist, he could point to discoveries or formulas he had developed. If he'd been a businessman, a banker, a lawyer, by now he'd have a fat bank account to retire on. But what did he have to show for his years of teaching? Two textbooks no longer used. A bunch of journal articles that nobody read. No, nothing palpable. He'd given his all for—what?

"Absolutely nothing, Hannah." George spoke, forgetting Hannah had not been reading his thoughts. "Absolutely nothing to show for all the years of classes, grading papers, lecture preparations, student conferences, committee meetings, professional course work. Oh, maybe an occasional letter from a student or someone wanting a recommendation. But nothing tangible after years of trying to get students to love philosophy and see its value, the need to know the value and power of ideas. How do you measure all that?"

Unaware of his action, George moved away from Hannah who remained seated on the edge of the chair as if she might have to leap up and rescue him at any moment.

"George, there's no way to measure the number of students who now see the importance of philosophy in their lives because of you and your love of teaching. Or, even how many of them have become teachers themselves because of you."

"Poor souls."

"You don't mean that. You've been very fortunate to find something you love to do and do well for so long. Some people spend their lives in jobs they hate or searching for one they love. What more could you want?"

"What more?" he whispered.

He stood swaying off balance for a moment while years of student faces, faces he'd forgotten, names forgotten, moments in time past, along with mixed voices echoing—great class, excellent teacher, best course ever, see life differently now, thanks for your help, learned so much, made me think, appreciate your patience— began rushing through his brain like a video tape on fast forward. For them. For you. For love. When the thought tape ran out, a slow, odorless fart that sounded like a sigh brought a smile to his face.

"George!"

He looked at Hannah, surprised. "You know, Hannah, that— that was a good one!"

"A good one?"

George saw concern on Hannah's face and went to her, bent down, and kissed her worried forehead. "Yes. It released a—a message."

"A message?"

"Yes, it's all making sense to me now. As a philosophy teacher I should have remembered the old dukkha of changing circumstances. Nothing lasts forever." George smiled. "Oh, Hannah. I've loved teaching so much I just forgot I couldn't do it forever."

"Oh?"

George touched the puzzled look on Hannah's face.

"Why, yes, yes. The air is clear now. You've helped me see that these, you know, are a sign, a metaphor, my enlightenment." George began pacing around the room.

"How could I, why should I, expect students to stay the same?" George, excited, began waving his arms. "No, I'm not the same, but I'm fighting to stay the same, to teach the same old way to students who aren't the same, but it doesn't work any more. I mean, my body's not the same. It's changing, wearing out, like my teaching, and you're right, flatulence is natural. And it's also natural for things to change, and so it's natural for students to say 'fuck' and wear earrings in their noses and on their nipples…"

"George?"

"…shave their heads, tattoo their butts, stick headphones in their ears, why, it's natural. I've been seeing things as I'd like them to be, not as they really are. Why, it's the contemporary philosophy of life, isn't it? They're products of mediocre television, movies, music, and the social nonsense of today. But I can't teach them if I can't love them, and I can't love them as I used to love them, and they can't love me, because I can't love them, and so in order to teach them I need to change so they can love me, but I can't change, so I should quit before it happens."

"George, are you okay? I'm not sure I'm following you. Before what happens?"

He looked at Hannah, surprised at her confusion.

"But don't you see? The farts are signals from my inner being trying to remind me of my old promise to quit teaching when I thought I was no longer effective, no longer loving my students.

And I'm not in love anymore with my students. I can't have student love affairs like I used to. I can't love like I used to. All I have left professionally is my dignity, my self-respect."

"Love affairs?" Hannah jumped up.

George noticed her flushed, apprehensive look. "Oh, don't look at me like that. You know what I mean, don't you? The farting's a reminder. Like that song says, 'it's the end of a love affair'." George tried to remember the melody for the lyrics.

"What love affairs?" Hannah's voice went up an octave, but George didn't notice.

"I don't know why I've been fighting it. I'm a perfect example of the Buddhist concept of confusion and delusion. Yes, you might even say I've reached an acknowledgement of sorts. I've perceived the truth of how things are without distortion or illusion. And you're right. Tomorrow, I'll notify them I'm retiring at the end of the term. After all the good years I've put in, I'm not going to wait around for the big one to destroy me. No, sir."

"The big one? Love affairs? George, what love affairs?"

Unaware of Hannah's perplexed stammering, George stopped pacing and plopped into his chair.

After putting on his reading glasses, he picked up his stack of student tests and flipped through them. After he picked one and began grading, he leaned slightly to one side and farted. He had a huge smile on his face that Hannah hadn't seen in quite a while.

"George? George!"